THE NATIONAL
MONEY LAUNDERING STRATEGY
FOR 2000

MARCH 2000

March, 2000

Foreword

When we unveiled the first *National Money Laundering Strategy* last year, we sent a clear signal that our approach toward this vital issue had changed fundamentally. The *1999 Strategy* was premised on the idea that money laundering threatened not only the United States by facilitating drug trafficking, organized crime, international terrorism, and other crimes, but that it also posed a threat in and of itself, by tainting our financial institutions and undermining confidence in parts of the international financial system. The *1999 Strategy* therefore outlined a comprehensive, integrated approach to combating money laundering, at home and around the world, through both law enforcement and banking supervision, with government policies and public-private partnerships.

The *National Money Laundering Strategy for 2000* provides a clear, detailed plan for government action this year. The *Strategy* builds on last year's strong foundation by announcing the conclusions of several high-priority interagency policy reviews and by providing a road map for future initiatives. The *2000 Strategy* also contains over sixty separate action items designed to combat money laundering on a broad range of fronts. These action items include efforts to strengthen domestic enforcement, to enhance measures taken by banks and other financial institutions, to build stronger partnerships with state and local governments, to bolster international cooperation, and to work with the Congress to give the Treasury and Justice Departments critical new tools to combat international money launderers and the foreign jurisdictions that offer them no-questions-asked banking services.

We are committed to ensuring that the action items in the *2000 Strategy* are implemented with vigor and dispatch. Therefore, every action item now includes a designation of the government office who is accountable for its implementation and for meeting specified goals and milestones. Implementation will be overseen by the Money Laundering Steering Committee, co-chaired by Deputy Secretary of the Treasury Stuart Eizenstat and Deputy Attorney General Eric Holder.

In his State of the Union last month, President Clinton spoke of the need to go after the one thing criminals value most -- their money. The *National Money Laundering Strategy of 2000* is our blueprint for doing just that.

Lawrence H. Summers
Secretary of the Treasury

Janet Reno
Attorney General

Table of Contents

Glossary of Abbreviations

AFMLS . . . . Asset Forfeiture and Money Laundering Section, Department of Justice

APEC . . . . Asia Pacific Economic Cooperation

APG . . . . Asia Pacific Group on Money Laundering

ATF . . . . Bureau of Alcohol, Tobacco and Firearms, Department of the Treasury

BJA . . . . Bureau of Justice Assistance, Department of Justice

BSA . . . . Bank Secrecy Act

BMPE . . . . Black Market Peso Exchange

C-FIC . . . . Financial Crime-Free Communities Support Program

CFTC . . . . Commodity Futures Trading Commission

CHFI . . . . Committee on Hemispheric Financial Issues

CMIR . . . . Currency or Monetary Instrument Report

CTR . . . . Currency Transaction Report

DEA . . . . Drug Enforcement Administration, Department of Justice

EOUSA . . . . Executive Office of United States Attorneys, Department of Justice

FATF . . . . Financial Action Task Force on Money Laundering

FBAR . . . . Foreign Bank Account Report

FBI . . . . Federal Bureau of Investigation, Department of Justice

FDIC . . . . Federal Deposit Insurance Corporation

Fed . . . . Federal Reserve Board

FinCEN . . . . Financial Crimes Enforcement Network, Department of the Treasury

FIU . . . . financial intelligence unit

FSF . . . . Financial Stability Forum

GCC . . . . Gulf Cooperation Council

GTO . . . . Geographic Targeting Order

HIDTA . . . . High Intensity Drug Trafficking Area

HIFCA . . . . High Intensity Money Laundering and Related Financial Crime Area

IEEPA . . . . International Emergency Economic Powers Act

ILEA . . . . International Law Enforcement Academy

INCSR . . . . International Narcotics Control Strategy Report

IFI . . . . international financial institution

INL . . . . Bureau for International Narcotics and Law Enforcement Affairs, Department of State

IRS-CI . . . . Internal Revenue Service -- Criminal Investigations, Department of the Treasury

IMF . . . . International Monetary Fund

MLCA . . . . Money Laundering Control Act of 1986

MLCC . . . . Money Laundering Coordination Center, U.S. Customs Service, Department of the Treasury

MLSA . . . . Money Laundering Suppression Act of 1994

Executive Summary

Last September, the Administration released its first *National Money Laundering Strategy*, a wide-ranging plan that set forth several dozen action items designed to advance four broad goals: strengthening domestic enforcement; enhancing the engagement of banks and other financial institutions; providing more effective assistance to state and local counter money laundering efforts; and bolstering international cooperation.

Money laundering -- the process of introducing the proceeds of crime into the legitimate stream of financial commerce by masking their origin -- is a global phenomenon of enormous reach. Money laundering may look like a clever game, but there is a dark, often bloody reality at its core. The same technology that allows legitimate capital to travel around the world in seconds is now routinely put to use by sophisticated money launderers. While no hard numbers exist on the amount of worldwide money laundering, former IMF Managing Director Michel Camdessus has estimated the global volume at between two and five per cent of the world's gross domestic product – some $600 billion even at the low end of the range.

The fight against money laundering is crucial for three basic reasons. First, counter-money laundering efforts allow us to pursue those who commit the underlying crimes that produce dirty money in the first place -- whether drug dealing, fraud, corruption, or other forms of organized crime. Second, money laundering facilitates foreign corruption, undermining U.S. efforts to promote democratic political institutions and stable vibrant economies abroad. Finally, counter-money laundering efforts help us defend the integrity of our financial system and institutions against the corrupting influence of ill-gotten gains.

Now, some six months later, we are issuing the *National Money Laundering Strategy for 2000*, which complements and expands upon last year's document. It reports on the conclusions of studies and initiatives called for in the *1999 Strategy*, discusses our objectives for this coming year, and sets forth a broad array of action items organized in a consolidated, government-wide plan. The *2000 Strategy* also sets goals and milestones to be achieved along the way.

In particular, the *2000 Strategy*:

(1)   designates the first four High Risk Money Laundering and Financial Crime Areas (HIFCAs) and launches the C-FIC state and local grant program;

(2)   proposes legislation providing the Secretary of the Treasury with new discretionary authorities to crack down on foreign jurisdictions, institutions or classes of transactions found to pose a serious money laundering threat;

(3)   calls for the passage of legislation submitted last year giving prosecutors and investigators important new tools to combat money laundering, including by designating foreign corruption as a money laundering predicate offense;

(4)   announces a final rule on applying suspicious activity reporting (SAR) requirements to money service businesses, and announces a plan to issue this year final SAR rules for casinos and proposed SAR rules for brokers and dealers in securities;

(5)   articulates a new method for identifying countries that pose serious threats;

(6)   details Administration plans for issuing guidance to financial institutions to apply enhanced scrutiny to certain high-risk accounts; and

(7)   calls for two important studies on the appropriate role of "gatekeepers" to the global financial system, such as lawyers and accountants.

The key items of the *Strategy*, arranged by Goal, are as follows:

Goal 1:   ***Strengthening Domestic Enforcement to Disrupt the Flow of Illicit Money***

   • Oversee specially-designed counter-money laundering efforts in newly designated High Risk Money Laundering and Financial Crime Areas (HIFCAs). Three geographical areas -- New York/Northern New Jersey, Los Angeles, and San Juan -- and one money laundering system, bulk cash smuggling across the Southwest border, have been designated.

   • Call for enactment of money laundering legislation that would give prosecutors and investigators important new tools, including the expansion of the list of predicate offenses to include numerous foreign crimes -- including public corruption -- and creating a new criminal offense of bulk cash smuggling.

   • Enhance interagency coordination of money laundering investigations against major money laundering systems such as the bulk cash movement of currency between the United States and Mexico, and the Black Market Peso Exchange System.

   • Enhance the capacity of the Justice Department's Special Operations Division to contribute to financial investigations in narcotics cases.

   • Make the Customs Service's Money Laundering Coordination Center (MLCC) fully operational with the participation of all relevant law enforcement agencies, and enhance

2

the MLCC's coordination of investigative efforts against the Black Market Peso Exchange System.

- Enhance the money laundering focus of counter-drug task forces.

- Under the guidance of the Office of Management and Budget, undertake a thorough review of resources devoted to anti-money laundering efforts.

Goal 2: ***Enhancing Regulatory and Cooperative Public-Private Efforts to Prevent Money Laundering***

- Develop guidance for financial institutions to subject high-risk accounts and transactions to enhanced scrutiny. Such guidance will be the product of consultations with the financial services industry, privacy advocates, the law enforcement community and the Congress.

- Update federal bank supervisory agencies' examination procedures to ensure that they are risk-focused, with increased emphasis on identifying those institutions that are most susceptible to money laundering.

- Educate money services businesses about their obligations under new rules requiring them to register and report suspicious activity.

- Issue a final rule for the reporting of suspicious activity by casinos and card clubs.

- Propose rules for the reporting of suspicious activity by brokers and dealers in securities.

- Expand the flow to banks of information based on SARs and other BSA reports, and on the utility of these reports to law enforcement.

- Identify issues raised by the use of professionals, including accountants, auditors and lawyers, by money launderers and other financial criminals, and develop recommendations to address these issues.

- Recommend modifications to existing counter-money laundering laws and regulations, as necessary, to enhance the protection of personal information obtained to carry out these counter-money laundering programs.

Goal 3: ***Strengthening Partnerships With State and Local Governments to Fight Money Laundering Throughout the United States***

- Accept applications and award grants under the C-FIC program.

- Promote the use of FinCEN's Gateway Program as a vehicle for two-way information exchange and joint state-federal financial analysis projects.
- Reach out to state and local authorities broadly for contributions to the *National Money Laundering Strategy.*

Goal 4:   ***Strengthening International Cooperation to Disrupt the Global Flow of Illicit Money***

- Propose legislation giving the Secretary of the Treasury discretionary authority to take calibrated action against international money laundering threats, including by prohibiting U.S. financial institutions from maintaining correspondent accounts with designated foreign financial institutions or jurisdictions.

- Identify jurisdictions that pose a money laundering threat to the United States, both through an internal evaluation process and participating in the work of the Financial Action Task Force to identify financial crime havens.

- Use our available authorities to take appropriate action with respect to identified financial crime havens, including issuance of bank advisories when appropriate.

- Support efforts, including that of the OECD, to identify tax havens.

- Work toward universal implementation of the FATF 40 Recommendations, and promote the development of FATF-style regional bodies.

- Develop initiatives to address the problem of foreign government officials who systematically divert public assets to their personal use.

- Provide training and technical assistance to nations making efforts to implement counter-money laundering measures.

- Urge the international financial institutions to explore mechanisms to encourage and support countries, in the context of financial sector reform programs, to adopt anti-money laundering policies and measures.

Background

Money laundering is relatively simple to describe, but difficult to investigate and prosecute. In particular, someone who conducts a financial transaction with knowledge that the funds or property involved in the transaction are the proceeds of crime, and who intends to further that crime, or to conceal or disguise those proceeds, is laundering money.[1] The funds to be laundered can be generated by a wide variety of criminal activity -- from narcotics trafficking and extortion, to fraud and corruption -- because most crimes are committed for profit, and the profits must be laundered to be used. These criminal proceeds can originate anywhere in the world and take many forms.

In enacting the Money Laundering and Financial Crimes Strategy Act of 1998, Congress recognized the need to address the threat of money laundering comprehensively. Combating money laundering is important for three reasons:

- First, money laundering is a crucial adjunct to the underlying crime that generate the money, whether drugs, fraud or other forms of crime.

- Second, money laundering helps foreign corrupt officials disguise misappropriated public assets -- often assets provided by the United States to improve the lives of their countries' citizens.

- Third, counter-money laundering helps us defend the integrity of our financial system and institutions against the corrupting influence of ill-gotten gains.

Money Laundering as an Adjunct to Underlying Crimes

Money laundering provides the fuel that allows drug traffickers, arms dealers, terrorists, and others to conduct their criminal business. In his 1995 remarks to the United Nations on the Occasion of the 50th Anniversary of its Creation, President Clinton said:

> Criminal enterprises are moving vast sums of ill-gotten gains through the international financial system with absolute impunity. We must not allow them to wash the blood off profits from the sale of drugs, from terror, or from organized crime.

---

[1] The Money Laundering and Financial Crimes Strategy Act of 1998, Pub. L. 105-310 (October 30, 1998) (the "1998 Strategy Act"), which calls for a national money laundering strategy, describes "money laundering and related financial crimes" as "the movement of illicit cash or cash equivalent proceeds into, out of, or through the United States, or into, out of, or through United States financial institutions." See 31 U.S.C. 5340(2)(A).

These thoughts have been echoed by Secretary Summers, who has said: "The attack on money laundering is an essential front in the war on narcotics and the broader fight against organized crime worldwide. Money laundering may look like a polite form of white collar crime, but it is the companion of brutality, deceit and corruption."

The importance of money laundering to criminals creates opportunities for law enforcement to detect crime, as it forces criminals to interact with the commercial and financial sectors. As investigators "follow the money" they find useful hooks with which to catch those who commit the underlying crimes.

Enforcement experts divide the process of money laundering into three stages:

1. *Placement*. Placement means putting the illicit funds into the financial system. In the case of currency paid for illegal narcotics, the need is obvious. Currency is anonymous, but it is difficult to handle, hard to hide, takes time to move, and attracts attention. If a crime generates non-currency proceeds (for example, the proceeds of a fraudulent stock sale or public corruption), placement occurs when the proceeds first come under the criminal's control.

2. *Layering*. The launderer's job is not finished when money is placed. Large amounts of unexplained value tend to attract attention. Funds must be moved and broken up to hide their true origin and to suggest a legitimate source. This process is called "layering." Through layering, the launderer can move funds from one nation, financial institution, or form through two or three others in a matter of moments, given the speed at which transactions can now be conducted via high-speed computer networks.

3. *Integration*. Once funds are layered sufficiently, they can be put to use by the criminals who have control over them. The funds are now no longer being moved simply to obscure their origin and true ownership but to finance the criminal's activities.

This movement of money through the financial system leaves a trail. If that trail can be uncovered, it identifies those who deliberately, through willful blindness or through negligence, facilitate and finance crime. The trail can also lead back to the drug dealers, arms traffickers, swindlers, or others whose crimes generated the money.

Today, more than ever before, money laundering is a world-wide phenomenon and an international challenge. We do not have a precise estimate of the amount of money laundered each year in the United States or internationally, though efforts are underway to improve our ability to make such a measurement. It is, however, possible to get a rough picture of the problem. Former IMF Managing Director Michel Camdessus has estimated that the volume of cross-border money laundering is between 2 and 5 percent of the world's gross domestic product. Even at the lower end of that range, the amount of the proceeds from narcotics trafficking, arms trafficking, bank and securities fraud, counterfeiting, and other similar

6

crimes laundered worldwide each year amounts to almost $600 billion. In light of American financial institutions' prominent role in the international financial system, a substantial portion of that $600 billion is likely laundered through the United States. And even a fraction of that amount, reinvested year after year, generates a massive war chest of criminal capital.

Money Laundering's Relation to Foreign Corruption

As noted above, money laundering often enables corrupt foreign officials to systematically divert public assets to their personal use, which in turn undermines U.S. efforts to promote democratic political institutions and stable, vibrant economies abroad. The relationship between money laundering and corruption was recognized at the G-8 Ministerial Conference on Combating Transnational Organized Crime, held in Moscow in October, 1999, when Attorney General Reno and other Justice Ministers issued a Communique stating that the fight against money laundering "will help ensure an environment which promotes official integrity and is intolerant of corruption."

Money Laundering as a Corrupting Influence on Financial Systems and Institutions

Money laundering taints our financial institutions, and, if unchecked, can undermine public trust in their integrity. President Clinton underscored this point in announcing Presidential Decision Directive 42 (PDD-42) when he stated that much of the problem posed by international organized crime "stems from the corrosive effect on markets and governments of their large illegal funds." In an age of rapidly advancing technology and globalization, the uncontrolled laundering of large sums can disturb financial stability.

* * * * * * * *

It is the goal of the United States to ensure that criminals and their laundered money can find no safe haven anywhere and to destroy criminal organizations by taking the profit out of crime. The increased threat from international organized crime, coupled with the globalization of our economy and the explosion of communications technology, requires our anti-money laundering efforts to be multi-dimensional. And they are. At the federal level, our nation's efforts to combat money laundering involve the coordinated work of a broad array of federal agencies implementing the Money Laundering Control Act[2] and the Bank Secrecy Act.[3] The Treasury and Justice Departments lead the law enforcement effort, while the federal financial regulatory agencies -- the Federal Reserve Board, the Office of the Comptroller of the Currency, the Federal Deposit Insurance Corporation, the Office of Thrift

---

[2] Pub. L. 99-570, Title XIII (October 27, 1986), as amended, codified at 18 U.S.C. 1956 and 1957.

[3] Pub. L. 91-508 (October 26, 1970), as amended, codified at 12 U.S.C. 1829b, 12 U.S.C. 1951-59, and 31 U.S.C. 5311-5330.

Supervision, the National Credit Union Administration, and the Securities and Exchange Commission -- are responsible for the examination of the financial institutions within their respective jurisdictions to ensure that those institutions have created effective internal systems to detect potential money laundering.

A detailed description of the laws and regulations that these agencies enforce, and the complimentary efforts of the state and local governments in the counter-money laundering effort, appears at Appendix 1.

As the volume of goods, services, and funds crossing our borders grows, government must fight not only the crimes against ordinary citizens from which dirty money derives, but also the threats posed by the laundering of those funds -- threats to trade, the integrity of financial institutions, and, ultimately, to national security. This second *National Money Laundering Strategy* details our efforts to do just that.

Goal 1: Strengthening Domestic Enforcement
To Disrupt the Flow of Illicit Money

The *1999 Strategy* identifies as its first goal the intensification of enforcement efforts to disrupt the flow of illicit money in the United States, and several important steps have been taken in the months since the *1999 Strategy's* release. Most significantly, the first High Intensity Money Laundering and Related Financial Crime Areas (HIFCAs) are being announced in this *Strategy*, and efforts are underway to establish action teams in each of these areas to target money launderers for prosecution. Anti-money laundering enforcement efforts, however, have not been limited solely to HIFCAs. Secretary of the Treasury Summers and Attorney General Reno have issued a joint memorandum to U.S. Attorney's Offices and federal law enforcement field offices throughout the country, communicating the importance of money laundering enforcement and emphasizing necessary steps to be taken. Additionally, we have commenced discussions with relevant industry leaders to combat the Colombian Black Market Peso Exchange (BMPE), and have enhanced the capabilities of the Justice Department's Special Operations Division (SOD) and the Customs Service's Money Laundering Coordination Center (MLCC) to target money launderers more effectively.

Much work, however, remains to be done, and strengthening federal enforcement of the money laundering laws remains the first goal of the *2000 Strategy*. In the coming year, HIFCA action teams will become operational and begin intensive efforts against money laundering in their respective areas. In the meantime, the HIFCA Working Group in Washington will monitor the action teams' progress, and will begin the process of new HIFCA designations for 2001, including the establishment of a formal application process for state and local governments and law enforcement. Additionally, continued progress will be made in enhancing the efficiency and effectiveness of anti-money laundering enforcement, including more effective use of Suspicious Activity Reports (SARs) and other Bank Secrecy Act (BSA) information.

In sum, the Action Items below represent a continued concerted federal effort to identify money launderers and money laundering areas within the United States, and to take aggressive enforcement action against them.

Objective 1: Concentrate Resources in High-Risk Areas

A centerpiece of the *1999 Strategy's* federal enforcement initiatives, HIFCAs will concentrate law enforcement efforts at the federal, state, and local level to combat money laundering in high-intensity money laundering zones, whether based on drug trafficking or other crimes. The designation of HIFCAs is required by statute.[4] The statute mandating HIFCAs sets forth an extended list of factors that must be

---

[4] Designation of HIFCAs as part of the *National Strategy* is required by the 1998 Strategy Act. See 31 U.S.C. 5341(b)(8) and 5342(b).

considered in designating a HIFCA. These factors encompass three general categories of information:

1. demographic and general economic data;

2. patterns of BSA filings and related information; and

3. descriptive information identifying trends and patterns in money laundering activity and the level of law enforcement response to money laundering in the region.

It is not a requirement that HIFCAs be defined geographically. They can also be created to address money laundering in an industry, sector, or a financial institution or group of financial institutions.

DESIGNATIONS FOR THE YEAR 2000

Upon the issuance of the *1999 Strategy*, the Treasury and Justice Departments led a process to identify and designate the first HIFCAs. As part of this process, the two Departments convened the HIFCA Working Group to collect and analyze all relevant information. The HIFCA Working Group, co-chaired by the Justice Department Criminal Division and the Financial Crimes Enforcement Network (FinCEN), included representatives from the U.S. Customs Service, the Internal Revenue Service-Criminal Investigations (IRS-CI), the U.S. Secret Service, the Federal Bureau of Investigation (FBI), the Drug Enforcement Administration (DEA), the U.S. Postal Inspection Service (USPIS), the Executive Office for United States Attorneys (EOUSA), the Executive Office for the Organized Crime and Drug Enforcement Task Forces, and the Office of National Drug Control Policy (ONDCP).

The HIFCA Working Group collected from each participating agency information concerning the nature and extent of money laundering activity in regions throughout the country, the number of investigations and prosecutions in the regions, the location of existing task forces addressing money laundering and financial crime, the law enforcement resources available in these regions and other information that would help identify HIFCA candidates.[5] This information was combined with an analysis of BSA data and demographic information.

Based on the recommendation of the Working Group, we are designating the following areas as the first

---

[5] The HIFCA Working Group regarded a high concentration of money laundering law enforcement activity in a geographic area as a factor supporting a HIFCA designation because (i) a primary purpose of the HIFCA program is to coordinate and enhance the focus of the anti-money laundering activities of ongoing task forces and federal, state, and local law enforcement investigations, and (ii) it indicates a local recognition of a money laundering problem and a commitment to combat that problem.

HIFCAs:

1. New York/Northern New Jersey Region

A. Demographic/Economic Information

The New York/Northern New Jersey region is the most populous urbanized area in the country. It is also the world's leading financial center, serving as headquarters for the New York Stock Exchange and 44 of the fifty major banks. This region is the home of three major airports, including JFK Airport, which is ranked fifth in the country for cargo and sixteenth for passenger traffic. Also located in the region is the Port of New York/New Jersey, the largest port complex on the East Coast of North America.

B. BSA Filings

The New York metropolitan area leads the nation in the number of SARs. In fiscal years 1998 and 1999, more than 14,000 SARs, with an aggregate reported dollar amount in excess of $33 billion, were filed in this area. In addition, in fiscal years 1998 and 1999 the State of New York had the second highest number of Currency Transaction Report (CTR) filings in the country, with the amount of money reported in the CTRs being the highest for any state. The New York metropolitan area had the third-highest number of inbound Currency or Monetary Instrument Report (CMIR) filings and the second-highest number of outbound CMIR filings. In both cases, New York has the highest dollar amounts reported in the CMIR filings.

C. Law Enforcement Activity

As a result of being a major financial center, the New York/Northern New Jersey area is already the focus of substantial law enforcement activity targeted against money laundering. Additionally, New York is the primary distribution center in the Northeast for cocaine and heroin. All law enforcement agencies are investigating major cases in this area; undercover investigations, in particular, indicate a great deal of money laundering activity. The United States Attorneys' Offices in this region (Southern District of New York, Eastern District of New York and District of New Jersey) filed money laundering charges (violations of 18 U.S.C. 1956 and 1957) against 190 defendants in 83 cases in fiscal year 1998.

Additionally, the New York/Northern New Jersey area has been designated as a High Intensity Drug Trafficking Area (HIDTA), and participates in the El Dorado Task Force, an initiative consisting of 195 federal, state, and local law enforcement personnel that seeks to identify, disrupt, and dismantle narcotics money laundering systems.

2. Los Angeles Metropolitan Area

A. Demographic/Economic Information

Los Angeles is the second largest city in the United States and is located only 150 miles from the Mexican border. Los Angeles has the largest number of financial institutions in the country and is also the largest manufacturing center in the country. The seaport of Los Angeles is one of the busiest on the West Coast and constitutes the largest container port in the United States.

B. BSA Filings

Los Angeles is also a major financial center, as demonstrated by the number of large filings under the BSA. In fiscal years 1998 and 1999, Los Angeles had the second highest number of SAR filings (5171), with the aggregate amount in excess of $7 billion. Also in fiscal years 1998 and 1999, Los Angeles had the highest number of outbound CMIRs and the second highest number of inbound CMIRs in the country. Finally, California had the highest number of CTR filings in the country in fiscal years 1998 and 1999.

C. Law Enforcement Activity

Federal, state and local law enforcement resources are highly concentrated on money laundering and financial crime in the Los Angeles area. An Organized Crime Drug Enforcement Task Force (OCDETF) District Coordination Group is located in Los Angeles. It has been designated as a HIDTA and has several HIDTA-funded task forces concentrating on drug money laundering, including the Southern California Drug Task Force.

In addition, Los Angeles has several task forces investigating non-drug financial crimes, including health care and telemarketing fraud. The FBI, IRS-CI, and the Customs Service each investigate a large number of major non-drug cases in the Los Angeles area which have money laundering components.

Investigative activity in fiscal year 1998 resulted in money laundering charges being filed against 197 defendants in 32 cases brought by the United States Attorney's Office for the Central District of California. The large number of money laundering and financial crime investigations and prosecutions in this district has resulted in the need for enhanced communication among agencies and coordination of efforts. Otherwise, the large number of cases will continue to result in high investigative and prosecutive thresholds, which unfortunately has resulted in a large number of potential cases that cannot be addressed by law enforcement at this time.

3. San Juan, Puerto Rico

A. Demographic/Economic Information

Puerto Rico's location in the Caribbean and its status with respect to the United States makes the island of great strategic importance with respect to drug trafficking, money laundering and financial crimes. The Caribbean region has become a focal point for both drug and non-drug money laundering. The proliferation of offshore financial crime havens in the Caribbean in the past decade have made this a region of great concern to the United States.

Puerto Rico is the Caribbean's most industrially developed island and is the transportation center of the Caribbean. The port of San Juan is the most active port of entry in the Caribbean and is the closest United States entry point for South American drug traffickers.

B. BSA Filings

In fiscal years 1998 and 1999, San Juan ranked ninth in the country for the volume of currency reflected on inbound CMIRs and eighth for volume of currency reflected on outbound CMIRs. Although banks in Puerto Rico filed 566 SARs totaling $627.7 million during fiscal years 1998 and 1999, San Juan banks filed only 45 SARs for $2.4 million. The apparent discrepancy between the large volume of reported currency flowing into and out of Puerto Rico, and the relatively small number and value of reported suspicious activities in Puerto Rico's financial center, will be a primary focus of the HIFCA action team. Further, San Juan ranks below only New York/New Jersey and Los Angeles for suspicious postal money order activity identified by USPIS.

C. Law Enforcement Activity

Puerto Rico has been the location of several major law enforcement anti-money laundering operations over the past five years, and has a high concentration of federal anti-money laundering law enforcement activity. San Juan has an OCDETF District Coordination Group, has been designated as a HIDTA, and has a HIDTA-funded Money Laundering Initiative in place which includes the Drug Smuggling/Money Laundering Interdiction Task Force.

4.   Cross-Border Currency Smuggling/Movement in Texas/Arizona to and from Mexico

This HIFCA designation focuses not simply on a geographic region, but on the system through which large volumes of currency (largely derived from drug trafficking) is smuggled or moved across the border between the United States and Mexico. As domestic money laundering enforcement improves, money launderers resort more frequently to the physical removal of the currency in bulk. This phenomenon is especially significant with respect to Mexico due to the ever-larger role that Mexican drug traffickers have carved out in the transportation of drugs into the United States. In fact, at this time the majority of Customs currency seizures for fiscal year 2000 have occurred along the Southwest border.[6]

> **Action Item 1.1.1:** **The Departments of the Treasury and Justice will oversee specially-designed counter-money laundering efforts in each newly designated HIFCA.**
>
> > **Lead:**[7] Assistant Secretary for Enforcement, Department of the Treasury.
> > Assistant Attorney General, Criminal Division, Department of Justice.
> >
> > **Goal for 2000:** Initiate joint federal, state, and local anti-money laundering efforts led by newly created or designated money laundering action teams.
> >
> > **Milestones:** During this year, the HIFCAs will establish or identify action teams. By December, the HIFCA Working Group will report to the Money Laundering Steering Committee on the overall progress made in the first four designated HIFCAs.

As noted above, the HIFCA program is intended to concentrate law enforcement efforts at the federal, state, and local level to combat money laundering in designated high-intensity money laundering zones. In order to implement this goal, a money laundering action team will be created or identified within each HIFCA to spearhead a coordinated federal, state, and local anti-money laundering effort. Each action team will:

- be composed of all relevant federal, state, and local enforcement authorities, prosecutors, and financial regulators;

- focus on tracing funds to the HIFCA from other areas, and from the HIFCA to other areas, so that related investigations can be undertaken;

- focus on collaborative investigative techniques, both within the HIFCA and between the HIFCA and other areas;

---

[6] The HIFCA Working Group recognizes that the movement of bulk cash is an area of concern along the whole of the Southwest Border, including the District of New Mexico and the Southern District of California. Information currently available to the working group indicates that the areas at greatest risk from the movement of such cash currently exist in Texas and Arizona. Clearly, the HIFCA will need the support of adjacent jurisdictions, especially if, as we anticipate, increased efforts in the HIFCA areas lead to a diversion of the illicit cash to other jurisdictions.

[7] Each Action Item within the *Strategy* identifies one or more "lead" officials. Leadership designations do not confer substantive authority and do not signify a limitation on participation by other relevant agencies.

- ensure a more systematic exchange of information on money laundering between HIFCA participants; and

- include an asset forfeiture component as part of its work.

In targeting identified money laundering mechanisms in its chosen area, each action team will draw together all available relevant information, including SAR information, for combined analysis.

During the course of the year, the HIFCA Working Group will work with the newly-designated HIFCAs to formulate a reporting and evaluation system so that the impact of the HIFCAs can be evaluated. By December, the HIFCA Working Group will report to the Money Laundering Steering Committee on the progress in the HIFCAs in the first year. The report will include a discussion of the extent of the involvement of state and local law enforcement agencies in the HIFCAs.

In order to concentrate law enforcement efforts on combating money laundering in HIFCAs, there must be a dedication of financial resources by the Departments of the Treasury and Justice. It is too soon to determine how the Departments should allocate counter-money laundering resources in these newly-designated HIFCAs. However, the Departments of the Treasury and Justice will develop a flexible plan to determine how best to allocate anti-money laundering resources as HIFCAs become operational. This issue will be addressed by the HIFCA Working Group, who will include in their December report to the Money Laundering Steering Committee a discussion of what resources have been and are planned to be allocated by law enforcement to ensure that HIFCAs receive high-priority allocations.

> ### Action Item 1.1.2: The Treasury Department in consultation with the Department of Justice will continue the process of evaluating and designating HIFCAs.
>
> **Lead:** Assistant Secretary for Enforcement, Department of the Treasury.
> Assistant Attorney General, Criminal Division, Department of Justice.
>
> **Goal for 2000:** Designate additional HIFCAs as appropriate.
>
> **Milestones:** By August, the Treasury Department will post on FinCEN's website the process by which localities can apply for HIFCA designation. An outreach effort to publicize the program to law enforcement and other officials will follow, and additional designations will be made as appropriate. An overall status report will be included in the *2001 Strategy.*

The HIFCAs designated in the *2000 Strategy* represent a new and innovative approach to money laundering enforcement. It will therefore be necessary to allow each of these HIFCAs to develop over the course of the year so that we can assess how the action teams operate prior to future designations.

Future HIFCAs will be selected from applications received from prospective areas, or from candidates proposed on the initiative of the Secretary of the Treasury or the Attorney General. The procedures for requesting a HIFCA designation will be developed within the next six months, and will be posted on the FinCEN website (www.treas.gov/fincen/). Though the specific procedures have not yet been finalized, a prospective applicant should expect to be required to submit an application to FinCEN that includes the following:

- a description of the proposed area or system to be designated,

- the focus and plan for the counter-money laundering projects that the designation will support, and

- the reasons such a designation is appropriate, taking into account the relevant statutory standards.

Measurement of the risk of money laundering activity in the area should be based both on local analysis and information and on relevant trend analysis. IRS-CI is now testing a pilot program designed to foster collection and analysis of such information. Agents assigned to this pilot program will be engaged in the collection, analysis, and dissemination of intelligence for field operations. This information will be utilized for trend reporting purposes and will be available to various law enforcement and regulatory agencies. The statistical information may also be used in the identification of money laundering risks in the HIFCA process.

Applications will be reviewed by the HIFCA Working Group, overseen by the Assistant Secretary of the Treasury for Enforcement and the Assistant Attorney General, Criminal Division, and the final selections will be made by the Secretary of the Treasury, in consultation with the Attorney General. Additionally, the HIFCA program will be publicized with state and local officials through an outreach effort.

Objective 2: *Communicate Money Laundering Priorities to Federal Law Enforcement in the Field*

The consequences of money laundering often far exceed the dollar value of specific money laundering violations. Money laundering investigations and prosecutions, including those money laundering operations that do not include large dollar amounts, serve to disrupt the illicit financial system that supports organized criminal activity, and safeguard the integrity of the financial system. Moreover, money laundering investigations can provide important derivative information to law enforcement, regulatory, and financial policy makers. It is therefore imperative for the Departments of the Treasury and Justice to communicate and emphasize to their investigative agents and prosecutors the importance of aggressively pursuing money laundering cases.

The *1999 Strategy* contains several Action Items calling for the Departments of the Treasury and Justice to communicate various priorities to the field in the form of joint memoranda. These have been combined into a single memorandum that was recently issued. It calls for:

- investigative and prosecutive thresholds to be made more flexible to allow for cases involving lower dollar amounts to be pursued if they offer the possibility of significant impact on a particular money laundering system;

- every federal district to consider establishing an interagency team to review SARs and coordinate follow-up investigations;

- agents and prosecutors to ensure that they debrief witnesses and informants for information concerning money laundering methods and techniques;

- law enforcement to use, when appropriate, electronic surveillance in money laundering investigations;

- emphasizing multi-district money laundering investigations, coordinated, when appropriate, through the Justice Department's Special Operations Division (SOD) or the Customs Service's Money Laundering Coordination Center (MLCC);

- U.S. Attorneys and law enforcement agency heads to ensure that agents and prosecutors are provided with adequate and regular training in financial investigations, financial analysis, and money laundering trends and techniques; and

- incorporating an asset forfeiture considerations at the inception of money laundering cases in order to help dismantle criminal organizations.

Action Item 1.2.1: The Departments of the Treasury and Justice will track implementation by investigators and prosecutors of the joint memorandum.

> **Lead:** Assistant Secretary for Enforcement, Department of the Treasury.
> Assistant Attorney General, Criminal Division, Department of Justice.

> **Goal for 2000:** Enhance the focus of federal field resources on money laundering investigations and prosecutions.

> **Milestones:** The Assistant Secretary and the Assistant Attorney General will track the field implementation of the joint memorandum's recommendations and report progress to the Money Laundering Steering Committee by November. Recommendations for further steps will be included in the *2001 Strategy*.

The Departments of the Treasury and Justice will continue to monitor their law enforcement agencies and prosecutors' offices to ensure that the recommendations in the joint memorandum are incorporated into their operations. By November, the Assistant Secretary and the Assistant Attorney General will make a progress report to the Money Laundering Steering Committee, along with recommendations on further actions that should be taken.

Objective 3: **Seek Legislation Enhancing Money Laundering Enforcement**

The United States has powerful statutory tools available to combat money laundering. However, as noted in the *1999 Strategy*, loopholes and missing pieces remain in our counter-money laundering structure. This objective discusses legislative provisions that address the enforcement of the money laundering laws, while Action Item 4.1.1 discusses legislative provisions that address international money laundering.

> **Action Item 1.3.1:** **The Administration will seek enactment of the Money Laundering Act of 2000 (formerly the Money Laundering Act of 1999), legislation with powerful provisions addressing domestic money laundering enforcement.**
>
> **Lead:** Assistant Attorney General, Office of Legislative Affairs, Department of Justice.
>
> **Goal for 2000:** Enactment of the Money Laundering Act of 2000.

The *1999 Strategy* articulated the Administration's intention to submit legislation aimed at enhancing the ability of law enforcement to investigate and prosecute domestic money laundering. This commitment was fulfilled on November 10, 1999, when the Administration submitted to Congress the Money Laundering Act of 1999. The Administration has continued to seek enactment of this legislation -- now the Money Laundering Act of 2000 -- and Assistant Attorney General Robinson testified in support of it on February 10th before the House Judiciary Committee's Subcommittee on Crime. The Money Laundering Act of 2000 includes the following important provisions addressing criminal money laundering enforcement:

- Expanding the BSA to create a new criminal offense of bulk cash smuggling in amounts exceeding $10,000, and authorizing the imposition of a full range of criminal sanctions when the offense is discovered. This provision will help prevent the flow of illicit cash proceeds out of the United States.

- Making it a criminal offense for a currency courier to transport more than $10,000 of currency in interstate commerce, knowing that it is unlawfully derived.

- Closing a legal loophole by making it clear that the federal money laundering statutes apply to both parts of a parallel transaction when only one part involves criminal proceeds. (For example, if a launderer moves drug money from Account A to Account B, and then replenishes Account A with the same amount of funds from Account C, the second transaction would also constitute money laundering.)

- Expanding the list of money laundering predicates to include numerous foreign crimes -- including arms trafficking, public corruption, fraud, providing material support to designated foreign terrorist organizations, and crimes of violence -- that are not currently covered by the money laundering statute. At present, for example, a foreign public official who accepts bribes or embezzles money and then launders the proceeds through a U.S. bank is not subject to a U.S. money laundering prosecution. The new provision will close that loophole, which severely limits the ability of the United States to investigate and prosecute the laundering of foreign criminal proceeds through financial institutions in the United States.

- Extending the civil penalty provision of the money laundering statute to give U.S. district courts jurisdiction over foreign banks that violate U.S. money laundering law, provided that the foreign bank maintains an account in the United States and that the bank receives appropriate service of process.

- Making it illegal to launder criminally derived proceeds through foreign banks. This provision would, for example, make it illegal for a person in the United States to send criminal proceeds abroad and launder them in a Mexican bank.

- Giving federal prosecutors greater access to foreign business records located in bank secrecy jurisdictions by providing sanctions when individuals in certain circumstances hide behind such foreign laws.

Action Item 1.3.2: The Administration will seek legislative authority for the Customs Service to search outbound mail.

> **Lead**: Assistant Commissioner for Congressional Affairs, U.S. Customs Service, Department of the Treasury.

> **Goal for 2000**: Enactment of legislation providing the Customs Service the same legislative authority to search outbound mail that it currently has to search inbound mail.

Currently, the Customs Service has the authority to conduct border searches without warrants in virtually every situation in which merchandise crosses the U.S. border. This authority extends to the searching of: (i) individuals entering and exiting the country; (ii) luggage entering and exiting the country; (iii) international mail entering and exiting the country that is sent through private carriers; and (iv) international mail entering the country that is sent through the U.S. mail. Outbound international letter-class mail is virtually the only means by which merchandise can be transported across the U.S. border without being subject to Customs inspection (unless a warrant is obtained). This unnecessary limitation of Customs' authority its efforts to deal comprehensively with the smuggling of currency out of the United States.

The Customs Service has long identified outbound international letter-class mail as a relatively safe and inexpensive means for criminals to transport currency out of the United States. Under Postal Service regulations, a letter-class mail parcel can weigh up to four pounds when mailed internationally (other than to Canada), and up to 60 pounds when mailed to Canada. A single four-pound letter-class parcel can accommodate approximately $180,000 in $100 bills.

To address this loophole, the Administration will continue to support legislation that would permit the Customs Service to search outbound international letter-class mail in cases where there is reasonable cause to suspect that the parcel contains monetary instruments, weapons of mass destruction, drugs, or merchandise mailed in violation of certain specified statutes. Such a provision would simply make Customs outbound authority parallel with its inbound authority. Customs would continue to be required to obtain a search warrant to inspect any domestic mail, or to read any correspondence contained in any international or domestic mail parcel.

Objective 4: **Examine the relationship between money laundering and tax evasion.**

> **Action Item 1.4.1:** **The Departments of the Treasury and Justice will study whether it would be advisable to expand the list of money laundering predicates to include tax offenses.**

> > **Lead:** Assistant Secretary for Tax Policy, Department of the Treasury.
> > Assistant Attorney General, Criminal Division, Department of Justice.
> > Assistant Attorney General, Tax Division, Department of Justice.

> > **Goal for 2000:** Develop recommendations on the advisability of expanding the list of money laundering predicates to include all or a specified subset of acts that constitute tax crimes.

> > **Milestones:** By May, a study group will be convened that will report its findings to the Money Laundering Steering Committee by November.

Tax evasion is a serious financial crime, and in some cases is closely related to money laundering. Yet tax evasion differs from money laundering in that tax offenses may involve legitimate income, while money laundering, by its very nature, almost always involves the movement of the proceeds of illegal activity. However, to determine whether it would be advisable to expand the list of money laundering predicates to include tax offenses, numerous issues need to be considered. Consequently, a study group will be assembled to analyze this issue and the results of this study will be reported to the Steering Committee.

Objective 5: Enhance Inter-agency Coordination of Money Laundering Investigations

The *1999 Strategy* acknowledges that the increasing globalization and sophistication of underground financial markets have hindered the effectiveness of money laundering investigations limited to single agencies or locations. As a result, the *1999 Strategy* calls for federal, state, and local authorities to develop an increasingly sophisticated capacity to track the implications of individual investigations and relate investigative efforts to one another. The Action Items below reaffirm that commitment.

> **Action Item 1.5.1:** **The Justice Department will continue to enhance the capacity of the Special Operations Division (SOD) to contribute to financial investigations in narcotics cases.**
>
> > **Lead:** Assistant Attorney General, Criminal Division, Department of Justice.
> >
> > **Goal for 2000:** The financial component of SOD will begin to identify and attack the financial underpinnings of major drug trafficking and drug distributing organizations and to coordinate multi-district cases against the financial operations of major drug traffickers.
> >
> > **Milestones:** By November, the Assistant Attorney General will report progress to the Money Laundering Steering Committee.

The SOD is a joint national coordinating and support entity initially comprised of agents, analysts, and prosecutors from the DEA, the FBI, the U.S. Customs Service, and the Criminal Division of the Department of Justice. Its mission is to coordinate and support regional and national-level criminal investigations and prosecutions of major criminal drug-trafficking organizations threatening the United States. This mission is routinely performed across both investigative agency and jurisdictional boundaries. Where appropriate, state and local investigative and prosecutive authorities are fully integrated into SOD-coordinated drug enforcement operations. The SOD coordination process has repeatedly demonstrated its effectiveness against the major drug trafficking and distribution networks.

In 1999, the original SOD approach was expanded to include a financial component that brings together all available information to identify and target the financial infrastructure of SOD targets, assists in coordinating investigations and prosecutions, and assists in seizing and forfeiting the proceeds, assets, and instrumentalities of these major drug trafficking organizations. The new component has been expanded to include IRS-CI. During the next year, the Department of Justice will continue to enhance the capacity of SOD to identify and attack the financial underpinnings of major drug trafficking and drug distributing organizations, and will begin coordinating multi-district cases against the financial operations of these organizations.

> **Action Item 1.5.2:** **The Customs Service will make the Money Laundering Coordination**

Center (MLCC) fully operational with the participation of all relevant law enforcement agencies.

> **Lead:** Assistant Commissioner for Investigations, U.S. Customs Service, Department of the Treasury.

> **Goal for 2000:** Full federal law enforcement participation in the MLCC.

> **Milestones:** By April, the DEA, IRS, FBI and OFAC will participate in the MLCC, and the deconfliction center will be available to all participating operations. The participation of the Postal Inspection Service will also be sought. By June, the MLCC will establish a working group of member agencies to review and enhance the procedures and protocols of the program.

The MLCC was created by the Customs Service, with assistance from FinCEN, in 1997. It serves as a repository for all intelligence information gathered through undercover money laundering investigations and functions as the coordination and deconfliction center for both domestic and international undercover money laundering operations.

Regarding coordination, the MLCC tracks information on subjects, businesses, financial institutions, and accounts involved in money laundering investigations. MLCC's data base also incorporates trade data and import, export, and financial intelligence through the use of the Customs Service's Numerically Integrated Profiling System (NIPS) and the Macro-Analysis Targeting System (MATS). Investigators can use MLCC, for example, to determine whether a particular individual and corporation have been linked together in a previous undercover investigation. In addition, links between MLCC and FinCEN promise to increase further the availability and quality of information for detailed field and long-term analysis of money laundering patterns and operations.

MLCC also provides a deconfliction mechanism to ensure that different undercover operations are not crossing paths and investigating each other. This function is critical to enhance the safety of agents who pose as money launderers in sting operations because relevant enforcement agencies can be alert to the presence of undercover agents operating in the area. The MLCC's recently established deconfliction center is operational and accessible through software provided to Customs field offices. It has also been made available to the SOD.

Action Item 1.5.3: The Department of Justice will enhance the money laundering focus of counter-drug task forces.

> **Lead:** Assistant Attorney General, Criminal Division, Department of Justice.

> **Goal for 2000:** Enhance the ability of the OCDETF Program to capture and analyze information on the money laundering aspects of its investigations.

> **Milestones:** By November, the Assistant Attorney General will report to the Money Laundering Steering Committee the results of a mid-year review of effectiveness of the revised OCDETF forms in capturing information on the money laundering aspects of its investigations. Additionally, the Department of Justice will include a money laundering presentation in three OCDETF Regional Conferences.

The *1999 Strategy* called for the impact of HIDTAs and OCDETFs on money laundering to be enhanced by calling attention to potential money laundering mechanisms or leads uncovered in the course of narcotics investigations a part of the agenda of every HIDTA and OCDETF effort. Both the HIDTA and OCDETF programs have responded to this call.

In particular, the Department of Justice's OCDETF Program -- which has produced many of law enforcement's most successful investigations of narcotics money laundering -- in the past year has taken steps to ensure that the money laundering focus of its task forces is encouraged, and that information concerning the money laundering focus of these interagency investigations is captured and analyzed. The Department of Justice has revised the OCDETF case initiation and prosecution forms to capture more information about the nature of the money laundering organizations and methods utilized to launder drug proceeds both domestically and abroad. This additional information provides trend analysis and feedback to the field to ensure that the task forces are addressing the money laundering aspects of drug trafficking organizations. In addition, money laundering presentations will be included on the agendas of OCDETF regional conferences in order to inform federal agents and Assistant United States Attorneys about current initiatives and to stress the importance of the financial element of drug trafficking organizations.

Additionally, the HIDTAs have responded to the *Strategy* by restructuring existing enforcement initiatives to emphasize money laundering, and introducing new ones. The counter-money laundering efforts of relevant OCDETFs, HIDTAs, and HIFCA action teams will continue to be appropriately coordinated.

Action Item 1.5.4: The Treasury Department will evaluate areas or financial sectors where use of Geographic Targeting Orders (GTOs) may be appropriate.

> **Lead:** Assistant Secretary for Enforcement, Department of the Treasury.

> **Goal for 2000:** Evaluate the appropriate use of GTOs, especially in the context of the newly-designated HIFCAs.

> **Milestones:** By November, action teams will report to HIFCA Working Group on whether GTOs would be appropriate within their respective HIFCAs. The HIFCA Working Group will then report these results to the Secretary of the Treasury.

GTOs can be issued by the Secretary of the Treasury to alter the reporting and recordkeeping requirements imposed on financial institutions for 60 day periods. (See 18 U.S.C. 5326). In practice, orders substantially reducing thresholds (from $10,000 to $750) for reporting of cash payments by money transmission customers sending funds from the United States to Colombia and the Dominican Republic played a significant role in the El Dorado Task Force investigation of money transmitters in New York, New Jersey, and Puerto Rico.

GTOs can be especially useful tools for addressing and coordinating problems in several areas of the country simultaneously, including efforts by HIFCAs in appropriate circumstances. For example, the New York and New Jersey efforts involved three United States Attorneys Offices and federal judicial districts in one case, and four in another. In addition, investigators outside of the GTO areas can be alerted to look for the displacement of money from those areas and to follow up on the leads so created.

Objective 6:   *Identify and Target Major Money Laundering Systems*

Underground financial markets provide criminals an opportunity to conceal their proceeds, and ultimately to mingle them into the legitimate economy or to move them out of the country. The *1999 Strategy* identified the Black Market Peso Exchange (BMPE) as one such important underground financial market and called for extensive action against it.

The BMPE is the primary money laundering system used by Colombian narcotics traffickers in repatriating perhaps as much as $5 billion annually to Colombia. This is how it works:

First, a Colombian drug cartel arranges the shipment of drugs to the United States. The drugs are sold in the U.S. for U.S. currency which is then sold to a Colombian black market peso broker's agent in the United States. The U.S. currency is sold at a discount because the broker and his agent must assume the risk of evading the BSA reporting requirements when later placing the U.S. dollars into the U.S. financial system.

Once the dollars are delivered to the U.S.-based agent of the peso broker, the peso broker in Colombia deposits the agreed upon equivalent in Colombian pesos into the cartel's account in Colombia. At this point, the cartel has laundered its money because it has successfully converted its drug dollars into pesos, and the Colombian broker and his agent now assume the risk for integrating the laundered drug dollars into the U.S. banking system. This is usually accomplished through a variety of surreptitious transactions. Having introduced the dollars into the U.S. banking system, the Colombian black market peso broker now has access to a pool of laundered U.S. dollars to sell to Colombian importers. These importers then use the dollars to purchase goods, either from the U.S. or from other markets, which are transported to Colombia, often via smuggling, in order to avoid Colombian laws and customs duties.

The BMPE Working Group -- overseen by the Treasury Under Secretary for Enforcement -- brings together federal enforcement, banking, and other agencies in an effort to dismantle the BMPE system. The BMPE Working Group continues to develop comprehensive and integrated plans to attack the peso exchange system from several directions simultaneously. In addition, the BMPE Working Group's multi-agency representatives work to ensure that all available investigative, regulatory, and trade policy tools are brought to bear on this effort.

> **Action Item 1.6.1**: **The Department of Treasury will intensify and expand efforts to increase the business community's education and awareness of the Black Market Peso Exchange System.**
>
> > **Lead:** Deputy Assistant Secretary for Enforcement Policy, Department of the Treasury. Chief, Asset Forfeiture and Money Laundering Section, Department of Justice.
> >
> > **Goal for 2000:** Develop a Business-Government Outreach program to engage the business community in the attack on the BMPE.
> >
> > **Milestones:** By April, the Attorney General, Deputy Secretary and Deputy Attorney General will meet with senior officials of companies whose products are vulnerable to the BMPE system. Additionally by April, the Departments of the Treasury and Justice will identify major trade associations whose membership includes companies whose products are vulnerable to the BMPE system, and schedule presentations on the BMPE at their annual meetings. By June, the Customs Service's Money Laundering Coordination Center, utilizing trade and investigative data, will develop a program to identify U.S. exporters that continue to be manipulated by the BMPE system, and will focus outreach and education. By July, the BMPE Working Group will develop and implement a Business-Government Partnership Program designed to promote the business community's education and awareness of the BMPE system and to jointly develop programs that will insulate their companies from this money laundering system.

Essential to the continued operation of the BMPE is the peso brokers' ability to have drug proceeds deposited in the U.S. financial system and to use these proceeds to pay for U.S. trade goods that are then smuggled into Colombia. To dismantle the BMPE, we must reach out to the business community, particularly those sectors of industry whose products are vulnerable to this system, and engage them in our attack on the BMPE. We must intensify our efforts to educate the business community on the operation of the BMPE system and to make them aware of BMPE activity.

The creation of a business-government partnership is a critical piece of our strategy to disrupt the BMPE. The importance of this partnership will be emphasized when the Attorney General, Deputy Secretary and Deputy Attorney General meet in April with senior officials of companies whose products are vulnerable to the BMPE system. The purpose of the meeting will be to explain how the BMPE operates, outline efforts to eliminate it, and solicit views on public-private partnership efforts that might be taken to combat this form of money laundering. Moving forward, we will continue to solicit the business community's thoughts and suggestions on domestic and international measures that government and industry might undertake to combat the BMPE.

> **Action Item 1.6.2: Law Enforcement Agencies, working in conjunction with the Money Laundering Coordination Center, will continue to identify the methods used for placement of peso exchange funds into the financial system.**
>
> > **Lead:** Assistant Commissioner for Investigations, U.S. Customs Service, Department of the Treasury.
> >
> > **Goal for 2000:** Develop a procedure for conducting strategic intelligence to identify emerging trends in the BMPE placement system.
> >
> > **Milestones:** The U.S. Customs Service's Money Laundering Coordination Center (MLCC), will (i) by April conduct strategic analysis of operational and financial intelligence to identify the most common methods for placement of narcotics proceeds into the financial system, (ii) by May, complete an analysis of SARs and other BSA information that document alleged BMPE violations, and (iii) by August, identify the geographic areas of businesses and individuals that receive the bulk of BMPE dollars.

The peso broker must arrange for the placement of street currency into the financial system or for its bulk shipment out of the United States. Customs, FinCEN, USPIS, IRS-CI and other members of the BMPE Working Group will continue to analyze operational intelligence, postal money order data, SARs, and other BSA information in an effort to identify transaction patterns of money laundering organizations. The BMPE Working Group members will continue their outreach to alert both the business and banking industry of emerging trends in the BMPE and emerging money laundering systems.

> **Action Item 1.6.3: The Money Laundering Coordination Center will enhance coordination of investigative efforts against the peso exchange system.**

Lead: Assistant Commissioner for Investigations, U.S. Customs Service, Department of the Treasury.

Goal for 2000: Expand interagency coordination of BMPE.

Milestones: By August, the BMPE Working Group will establish interagency protocols for developing and forwarding potential BMPE investigative leads.

The Money Laundering Coordination Center will continue to collect and coordinate intelligence from operations involving peso exchange targets. As an outgrowth of the BMPE Working Group, the USPIS and Treasury Department's Office of Foreign Assets Control (OFAC) are now working in partnership with the MLCC to more readily identify and more fully exploit BMPE targets.

Action Item 1.6.4: The Administration will promote continued cooperation with the Governments of Colombia, Aruba, Panama, and Venezuela.

Lead: Deputy Assistant Secretary for Enforcement Policy, Department of the Treasury.

Goal for 2000: Establishment of an International BMPE Task Force of experts from Colombia, Aruba, Panama, Venezuela, and the United States that will examine the BMPE, as a money laundering system, with a view toward reporting its findings and recommending policy options to senior government officials from the respective jurisdictions.

Milestones: The first meeting of the Task Force should occur by June, with follow-on meetings in three to four month intervals. By October, the BMPE Task Force should be fully operational.

The U.S. Interagency BMPE Working Group brings together federal enforcement, banking, and related agencies in an effort to attack the peso exchange system. It oversees a comprehensive program to restrict the peso exchange system from several directions at once and to ensure that all available investigative, regulatory, and trade policy tools are used in that effort. This comprehensive program includes significant international initiatives, including close cooperation with Colombia. Cooperation between the U.S. and Colombia is critical to U.S. counter-narcotics policy and our strategy to combat narcotics-related money laundering. The importance of this bilateral relationship was demonstrated on January 10, 2000, President Clinton announced a $1.28 billion emergency aid program for Colombia.

The International BMPE Task Force will enhance the cooperation between the governments of Colombia, Aruba, Panama and the U.S. in combating the BMPE. The Task Force as proposed establishes another concrete step that all of the governments most directly affected by the BMPE can take to broaden communication and cooperation, including enhanced support for law enforcement efforts.

The Task Force would comprise a Senior Officials Group and an Experts Working Group. The Senior Officials Group would include senior level officials appointed by each participating country and will give overall policy direction. The Experts Working Group would include no more than six banking, law enforcement, financial, trade, academic, or commercial experts from each jurisdiction, meet at least four times, and report findings and recommendations to the Senior Officials Group no later than October 1, 2001.

Objective 7: *Enhance the Collection, Analysis, and Sharing of Information to Target Money Launderers*

The *1999 Strategy* notes that reports by financial institutions of apparently suspicious conduct -- SARs -- are a critically important tool in targeting money launderers and money laundering systems. Increased attention is being paid to reviewing these reports and maximizing their usefulness to law enforcement.

> **Action Item 1.7.1:** **The Departments of the Treasury and Justice will ensure that their bureaus provide feedback to FinCEN on the use of SARs and other BSA information.**
>
> > **Lead:** Under Secretary for Enforcement, Department of the Treasury.
> > Assistant Attorney General, Criminal Division, Department of Justice.
> >
> > **Goal for 2000:** Institute a regular process to ensure that the federal law enforcement users of SARs and other BSA information provide feedback to FinCEN on the use of the information.
> >
> > **Milestones:** By September, the Under Secretary and the Assistant Attorney General will report to Money Laundering Steering Committee on (i) how each law enforcement bureau provides feedback to FinCEN on the use of SAR and other BSA information, (ii) any problems or issues the bureaus have had in this area, and (iii) methods to resolve any identified problems.

The *1999 Strategy* acknowledged that an analysis of investigative agencies' various uses of SARs would result in an increase in the usefulness of SARs to law enforcement, and the overall effectiveness of the SAR system. This feedback would also help FinCEN and bank supervisory agencies to provide better SAR reporting in the future. However, such an analysis is possible only if all agencies who have access to reports provide FinCEN with timely information about the way the reports are used and the results achieved from their use. As directed by the Under Secretary of Enforcement in July 1999, the Treasury Department's law enforcement bureaus will implement procedures to capture concrete information about SAR usage. The milestones detailed above will ensure that law enforcement bureaus are providing the requested SAR information to FinCEN in a routine and effective manner.

Action Item 1.7.2: The Departments of the Treasury and Justice will review available technologies to determine the utility of developing a uniform procedure for conducting document exploitation.

> **Lead:** Assistant Attorney General, Criminal Division, Department of Justice.

> **Goal for 2000:** Develop an interagency consensus on the feasibility and utility of uniform procedures for conducting document exploitation.

> **Milestones:** By May, the Department of Justice will convene a working group to examine this issue and will report to the Money Laundering Steering Committee by November.

Law enforcement agencies have developed different approaches for handling, reviewing, and extracting information from the large amounts of documents involved in a financial crime investigation. The Departments of Justice and the Treasury will review available technologies and determine whether, among other things, it would be useful to a procedure to standardize financial spread sheets with data fields for money laundering and asset forfeiture issues, and whether it would be beneficial to make the system uniformly available to law enforcement agencies and U.S. Attorneys.

Objective 8:   Intensify Training

No single training course can prepare a federal agent or prosecutor to deal with money laundering and other financial crimes effectively in a rapidly changing environment. Thus, the *1999 Strategy* called for financial investigative training of law enforcement agents and prosecutors to be enhanced. This mandate has been implemented in two ways. First, the Departments of the Treasury and Justice have communicated to their field agents and prosecutors the importance of continued money laundering and financial investigative training. Second, the Departments of Treasury and Justice will continue to hold national and regional money laundering conferences to focus attention on money laundering and to provide a forum for the exchange of information and experiences among law enforcement agents, prosecutors, and policy makers.

> **Action Item 1.8.1: The Departments of the Treasury and Justice will continue to sponsor national and regional money laundering conferences.**

> > **Lead:** Assistant Secretary for Enforcement, Department of the Treasury.
> > Assistant Attorney General, Criminal Division, Department of Justice.

> > **Goal for 2000:** Provide a forum for federal prosecutors and investigators from around

the country who are engaged in counter-money laundering effort to exchange ideas and experiences, and to discuss money laundering trends and enforcement strategies.

Milestones: By November, the Departments of the Treasury and Justice will hold a national money laundering conference.

By November, the Department of Justice, together with the Treasury Department, will convene a national money laundering conference of investigators and prosecutors to discuss new money laundering trends and enforcement strategies. Two years ago, the Treasury and Justice Departments began conducting a series of national conferences to foster the exchange of ideas among investigators and prosecutors engaged in counter-money laundering efforts. These conferences will continue on a regular basis, and will focus on emerging issues affecting, for example enhancing the use and analysis of SARs. Each law enforcement agency will be offered the opportunity to actively participate in the development and organization of these conferences.

Objective 9: *Continue to Improve the Efficiency and Effectiveness of Resource Management Related to Anti-Money Laundering Efforts.*

Various anti-money laundering programs and initiatives are being pursued by departments and agencies throughout the executive branch. But the government as a whole has never undertaken a comprehensive review of its allocation of resources in this area. In order to deploy our resources most effectively, we must have a comprehensive knowledge of the level of resources devoted to these programs and initiatives. Working with the Departments of the Treasury and Justice, the Office of Management of the Budget (OMB) has initiated a review of money laundering programs and resources across the federal government. The preliminary results are attached at Appendix 6.

Action Item 1.9.1: Under the guidance of OMB, the interagency community will undertake a thorough review of resources devoted to anti-money laundering efforts.

Lead: Assistant Secretary for Management, Department of the Treasury.
Assistant Attorney General for Administration, Department of Justice.

Goal for 2000: Complete a first comprehensive budget review to identify the resources devoted to anti-money laundering programs. Begin a process to ensure that resources are appropriately and effectively allocated.

Milestones: During the Spring and Summer, OMB and the Money Laundering Steering Committee will identify administration priorities and relevant information regarding money laundering to be used in the formulation of the fiscal year 2002 President's Budget.

The President's 2001 budget includes a separate appropriations request in the amount of $15 million for the implementation of critical components of the *National Money Laundering Strategy*. The Treasury Department will administer the allocation of these resources to enable, among other things, enhanced strategic analysis and support for HIFCAs, multi-disciplinary task forces for high profile investigations, funding for the C-FIC grant program, increased electronic submission of BSA filings, and leadership and direction for international enforcement policy.

The strategic review of current resources allocated to anti-money laundering programs will provide additional information about what we are spending, where it is spent, and if we are spending it as effectively as possible. The primary purpose of this exercise is to inform the decision-making across the inter-agency community in the context of the 2002 budget build. Coupled with the solicitation of comments from law enforcement and HICFA action teams, appropriate changes can then be built into the *2001 Strategy*. The plan will consider and draw upon, as appropriate, all potential sources of funding.

Goal 2: Enhancing Regulatory and Cooperative Public-Private Efforts to Prevent Money Laundering

An effective regulatory regime and close cooperation between the public and private sectors are essential to our counter-money laundering efforts. The *1999 Strategy* recognizes that efforts to fight money laundering rest on denying money launderers easy access to the legitimate financial system. This, in turn, depends on the elimination of overly strict bank secrecy, promotion of standardized recordkeeping practices, reporting of large currency and potentially criminal transactions, and internal and external audit and examination. Such efforts cannot succeed without the cooperation of financial institutions such as banks, securities dealers, and money services businesses.

Striking the proper balance among the various, and at times competing, interests is a difficult and delicate task. We must take into account the public's interest in both privacy and in a sound financial system, society's interest in security from the criminal conduct that money laundering supports, and the financial community's interest that regulations and guidance be reasonable and cost-effective. For that reason, the *1999 Strategy* called for three working groups to be established to examine issues in the following areas: (i) guidance for financial institutions on high-risk customers and transactions, (ii) bank examination procedures relating to the prevention and detection of money laundering, and (iii) privacy. The *2000 Strategy* reports on the activities of these working groups, and describes the steps that they recommend for the future.

As promised in the *1999 Strategy*, the Treasury Department has now issued, in conjunction with this year's *Strategy*, the final rule for the reporting of suspicious activity by money service businesses. Additionally, the *2000 Strategy* outlines an ambitious set of goals for the upcoming year. These goals include issuing final rules for the reporting of suspicious activity by casinos, as well as a proposed rule on suspicious activity reporting by brokers and dealers in securities. Additionally, a working group has been established to encourage continued and expanded cooperation between financial regulators and law enforcement on money laundering issues. The government will also seek a dialogue with legal and financial professional associations to enlist these important market professionals in the fight against money laundering.

Objective 1: *Enhance the Defenses of U.S. Financial Institutions Against Abuse by Criminal Organizations*

The *1999 Strategy* identifies as a significant money laundering threat the movement of criminal funds generated elsewhere into the United States through electronic transmittals. These electronic transmittals often move in larger amounts than currency deposits, and are more easily disguised as legitimate international trade or investment transactions. In response to this threat, the *1999 Strategy* established two working groups to examine if bank examination procedures relating to money laundering need to be improved, and how banks themselves could give enhanced scrutiny to transactions or patterns of transactions that pose a heightened risk of concern of potentially illicit activity. These working groups have completed their reviews, the results and recommendations of which are discussed in this section.

> **Action Item 2.1.1:** **The Departments of the Treasury and Justice, and the federal bank regulators, will work closely with the financial services industry to develop guidance for financial institutions to conduct enhanced scrutiny of those customers and their transactions that pose a heightened risk of money laundering and other financial crimes.**
>
> > **Lead:** Deputy Secretary, Department of the Treasury.
> >
> > **Goal for 2000:** In consultation with the financial services industry, issue guidance for financial institutions to conduct enhanced scrutiny of those customers and their transactions that pose a heightened risk of the possibility of illicit activities, including money laundering, at or through their financial institution.
> >
> > **Milestones:** An outreach program will seek the views of the banking and financial services industry (including local, regional, national, and international institutions and organizations), privacy advocates, the law enforcement community, and Members of Congress. These views will help shape the final guidelines.

The *1999 Strategy* called upon the Departments of the Treasury and Justice to convene a high-level working group of federal bank regulators and law enforcement officials to examine what guidance would be appropriate to enhance financial institution scrutiny of potentially high-risk transactions or patterns of transactions. The working group concluded that the most appropriate means to address the issue of enhanced scrutiny by financial institutions of certain customers and their transactions would be to work with the financial services industry to develop guidance or sound practices for enhanced scrutiny that financial institutions (both bank and non-bank) could incorporate within their existing anti-money laundering and suspicious activity reporting regimes. The working group rejected the possibility of developing new regulations or seeking new laws.

In developing the guidance, we will explore how financial institutions should identify those categories of customers that the financial institution has reason to believe pose a heightened risk of the possibility of illicit activities, including money laundering, at or through the financial institution, and should apply an enhanced level of scrutiny for those customers. Current levels of scrutiny would continue to apply to the majority of customers.

We anticipate that the guidance will also include "red flags" that financial institutions should be aware of, such as the size, velocity and location of the transaction, as well as other factors that are being developed in connection with the *Strategy's* review of correspondent banking and determinations of "financial crimes havens." The guidance will also likely include discussions of such things as private banking and payable through accounts.

As part of the development of the enhanced scrutiny guidance, a multi-faceted outreach program will be implemented that will provide necessary information to the financial services industry and the public as to the need for such guidance, as well as provide for a forum in which the industry and public can provide comments and help shape the guidance. The program will include discussions with the banking and financial services industry (including local, regional, national, and international institutions) privacy advocates, the law enforcement community, and Members of Congress.

> **Action Item 2.1.2:** **The federal bank supervisory agencies will implement the results of their 180-day review of existing bank examination procedures relating to the prevention and detection of money laundering at financial organizations.**
>
> > **Lead:** Deputy Comptroller, Community & Consumer Policy Division, OCC, Department of the Treasury.
> >
> > **Goal for 2000:** Ensure that anti-money laundering supervision is risk-focused, with increased emphasis on identifying those institutions or practices that are most susceptible to money laundering.
> >
> > **Milestones:** Each federal bank supervisory agency will continue to review existing examination procedures and, where necessary, revise, develop and implement new examination procedures consistent with the goal identified above. By November, each federal bank supervisory agency will prepare a report of the actions taken with regard to the review of examination procedures and the OCC will prepare a summary report for the Money Laundering Steering Committee.

As directed in the *1999 Strategy*, the OCC chaired a working group of federal bank supervisory agencies to review existing bank examination procedures relating to the prevention and detection of money laundering at financial institutions. This review was focused primarily on the effectiveness of the revised examination procedures that were developed in accordance with the Money Laundering Suppression Act of 1994 (MLSA). The MLSA requires federal banking agencies to review and enhance their procedures to better evaluate banks' programs to identify money laundering schemes involving depository institutions.

In general, the working group concluded that although the revised procedures were working well, they could be improved by ensuring that each agency's approach to anti-money laundering supervision is risk-focused, with a particular emphasis on identifying those institutions or practices that are most susceptible to money laundering. Toward that goal, each banking agency either has or is developing procedures to address high-risk areas such as private banking, payable through accounts, and wire transfer activity. Additionally, each agency either has or is developing procedures to address new trends, such as electronic banking and foreign correspondent accounts. The following are examples of anticipated actions:

- The OCC will complete and implement an updated *Comptroller's Handbook for Bank Examiners* that will include a new requirement to perform transactional testing of high-risk accounts at every bank examination.

- The OCC will implement a program to target for examination those institutions that are considered most vulnerable to money laundering.

- FDIC has issued revised BSA/Anti-Money Laundering risk-focused examination procedures that incorporate enhanced guidance to bank examiners on high-risk activities. These procedures will be amended in 2000 to include guidance on foreign correspondent accounts. The FDIC and OCC continue to develop interagency anti-money laundering training modules, which will be completed in 2000.

- The Federal Reserve will implement new procedures that will, among other things, concentrate on ensuring that banks implement effective operating systems and procedures to manage operational, legal and reputational risks as they pertain to BSA/Anti-Money Laundering efforts; provide guidance on appropriate levels of enhanced scrutiny for high-risk customers and services; and increase emphasis on maintaining systems to detect and investigate suspicious activity throughout every business sector of a banking organization.

- OTS will assess the efficacy of its recently revised risk-focused BSA examination procedures, and will implement enhancements developed by bench-marking with other agencies.

Objective 2: Assure that All Types of Financial Institutions Are Subject to Effective Bank Secrecy Act Requirements

The *1999 Strategy* identifies as a weakness in our anti-money laundering regulatory regime the fact that depository institutions are subject to more stringent BSA requirements than other types of financial institutions. For example, only institutions under the jurisdiction of the federal bank supervisory agencies are required to file SARs. In response, the *1999 Strategy* calls upon Treasury to issue final rules requiring suspicious activity reporting by money services businesses and casinos, and to work with the SEC in proposing rules for suspicious activity reporting by brokers and dealers in securities. The action items below reflect the progress that has been made in this area, and reaffirm our commitment to accomplish each task by the end of this year.

Action Item 2.2.1: **The Treasury Department will begin the process to ensure that money services businesses (MSBs) are educated about their obligations under the new rule requiring their registration and the reporting of suspicious activity.**

Lead: Director, FinCEN, Department of the Treasury.

>**Goal for 2000**: Continue the outreach effort to identify and educate the industry on the registration and suspicious activity reporting requirements. Additionally, establish an MSB program office within the Office of Regulatory Compliance and Enforcement at FinCEN.

>**Milestones**: By mid-year a contract will be in place for an outreach effort that, although primarily focused on MSB registration, will be the springboard for identification and education of the MSB industry on the filing of SARs.

With the publication of this year's *Strategy*, FinCEN is issuing a final rule requiring suspicious activity reporting by MSBs, which transfer funds, or issue, sell or redeem money orders or travelers checks. In addition, in March FinCEN will publish guidance in the Federal Register that is designed to assist the affected industry in complying with the rule. Since August 20, 1999, when FinCEN issued a final rule calling for the registration of MSBs with the Department of the Treasury, FinCEN has met with representatives of the money services business industry, state regulators and law enforcement experts in money laundering investigations and prosecutions to begin the outreach effort and to solicit input on guidance to accompany the SAR rule and forms. Issuance of the final rule for suspicious activity reporting by MSBs will significantly expand the ability of law enforcement to focus its anti-money laundering efforts on illicit financial activity occurring through non-bank financial institutions. In addition, the rule will assist in leveling the playing field in SAR reporting for those institutions that provide financial services to the public.

Through the Office of Public Education at the Treasury Department, a contractor will be engaged to assist in identifying and educating the MSB community about the registration and reporting requirements. The contractor will work with the Treasury Department to ensure, among other things, that educational materials produced are the most effective and will assist the industry in complying with the new rules. The new registration and reporting rules will become effective at the end of 2001. By that time, through this outreach effort, we expect to have identified and educated this extensive industry on its responsibilities under the rules. At the same time, within the Office of Regulatory Compliance and Enforcement at FinCEN, a unit dedicated to continuing the education effort and to working with the industry to ensure compliance with the MSB rules will be established. Working in conjunction with its partners at the IRS, this unit will be responsible for ongoing outreach to the industry to maximize compliance.

>**Action Item 2.2.2**: **The Treasury Department will issue a final rule for the reporting of suspicious activity by casinos and card clubs.**

>>**Lead**: Director, FinCEN, Department of the Treasury.

>>**Goal for 2000**: Issue the final rule and a revised form for suspicious activity reporting.

In addition, revise a casino industry compliance guide for SAR reporting. Once the rule and form are issued, FinCEN will engage in a comprehensive outreach program with the casino and card club industries and with their state regulators.

Milestones: The final rule will be issued by August, and will be followed by guidance to the industry. It is anticipated that the rule will go into effect the following year. The proposed final form and instructions will be revised by October, and comments will be solicited through OMB notices. Also, revised guidance will be published and distributed before the final rule becomes effective.

On May 18, 1998, FinCEN published a proposed rule that would require casinos and card clubs subject to the BSA to report suspicious transactions. The proposed standards for reporting were similar to those in effect for banks, but with a lowered threshold of $3,000. A new form was developed -- Suspicious Activity Report for Casinos (SARC) -- and is currently utilized by Nevada casinos, which are already subject to a state requirement to file SARCs with FinCEN. Also, FinCEN prepared and distributed a report for the casino industry and its regulators, which discusses areas within a casino that are particularly vulnerable to money laundering abuse and provides a series of specific examples of transactions that may constitute suspicious activity. FinCEN conducted four regional hearings during the comment period.

FinCEN has now completed its review of the comments filed and the transcripts of the public hearings and is drafting a final SAR rule, which will be published by August, and will take effect the following year. FinCEN will also revise the SARC guidance report and SARC form at the time the final rule becomes effective. Once the rule is finalized, FinCEN will undertake a concerted outreach effort with the casino and card club industries and their state regulators to assist federal authorities in ensuring compliance with these new requirements.

> **Action Item 2.2.3**: **The Treasury Department will work with the SEC to propose rules for the reporting of suspicious activity by brokers and dealers in securities.**
>
> **Lead**: Director, FinCEN, Department of the Treasury.
>
> **Goal for 2000**: Issue a proposed rule and draft form for suspicious activity reporting by securities brokers and dealers (SAR-S), and compliance guidance for the industry. Additionally, continue the process of educating the industry about the need to develop systems to guard against and detect money laundering abuse by its customers.
>
> **Milestones**: By the end of the year, FinCEN will issue the proposed rule, draft SAR-S form, and industry compliance guidance.

For the past several years, FinCEN has been working with federal and state securities regulators and law enforcement, self-regulatory organizations and representatives from the securities industry to devise an effective and practical system to both detect and report suspicious transactions conducted by brokers and dealers. Special rules and systems need to be applied to the securities industry to ensure conformity with the existing examination and enforcement programs of securities regulators in recognition of the fact that the securities industry is generally not utilized in the money laundering "placement" stage because of near-universal policies against accepting currency for transactions. However, the services and products provided by the securities industry, including the efficient transfer of funds between accounts and to other financial institutions, the ability to conduct international transactions, and the liquidity of securities, provide opportunities for money launderers to obscure and move illicit funds.

Implementation of a SAR regime for the securities industry is an extension of FinCEN's broader effort to devise a comprehensive system of suspicious activity reporting for all significant providers of financial services. FinCEN, in consultation with the SEC and the industry's self-regulatory organizations, intends to issue a proposed rule requiring SAR reporting for the securities industry, together with a draft SAR-S reporting form and compliance guidance by the end of the year. Thereafter, it will hold at least three regional hearings to provide an opportunity for the industry to comment directly on the proposals.

> **Action Item 2.2.4**: **The IRS will enhance the resources devoted to conducting BSA examinations of MSBs and casinos.**
>
> > **Lead**: Assistant Commissioner for Examinations, IRS, Department of the Treasury.
> >
> > **Goal for 2000**: Determine whether IRS efforts are adequate to meet its responsibilities of ensuring MSB and casino compliance with the BSA.
> >
> > **Milestones**: The Treasury Department will hold a meeting with the IRS by August to review the IRS program. Based on this meeting, by November the IRS will identify for the Money Laundering Steering Committee priorities and concerns, and make recommendations on whether additional resources need to be devoted to the program.

The Secretary of the Treasury has delegated the responsibility to the IRS to examine certain nonbank financial institutions (*e.g.*, casinos and money services businesses) for compliance with BSA.[8] Just as the federal financial agencies do for banks, thrifts and credit unions, the IRS performs essential regulatory oversight of these institutions, including identifying institutions that are subject to BSA requirements, educating them regarding their BSA obligations, and conducting BSA compliance examinations. Therefore, it is necessary that the IRS ensure that it is adequately meeting these counter-money laundering responsibilities, especially given the new and future suspicious activity reporting requirements of the MSB and casino industries, respectively.

---

[8] See, 31 CFR Part103.46(b)(8) and Treasury Directive 15.41.

Action Item 2.2.5: **The Treasury Department will examine money laundering vulnerabilities of financial services providers not otherwise addressed in the *Strategy* -- such as the insurance industry, travel agencies, and pawn brokers -- and recommend, as appropriate, application of BSA requirements.**

> **Lead:** Director, FinCEN, Department of the Treasury.

> **Goal for 2000:** Initiate a review of financial service providers defined under the BSA to identify priorities for extending BSA requirements -- including suspicious activity reporting -- or taking other appropriate regulatory actions.

> **Milestones:** By the end of the year, a study group will examine actual and potential abuses of financial industry sectors not otherwise addressed in this *Strategy*. It will report its findings, including recommendations regarding the extension of BSA requirements to additional financial sectors, to the Money Laundering Steering Committee.

The BSA defines a range of financial institutions and industries that may be vulnerable to money laundering. Examples include the insurance industry, the travel industry, and pawn brokers, none of which have been subject to the full range of BSA requirements, particularly suspicious activity reporting requirements. With the recent enactment of the Gramm-Leach-Bliley Act, it is now appropriate to examine the entire range of financial service providers subject to the BSA to consider the extent to which money laundering vulnerabilities might be addressed through the expansion of suspicious activity reporting or other BSA requirements.

Objective 3: *Continue to Strengthen Counter-Money Laundering Efforts of Federal and State Financial Regulators*

The perspectives of law enforcement and regulatory officials are often different. Complementary approaches to counter-money laundering efforts require enhanced coordination between enforcement and regulatory officials. Recognizing this fact, the Treasury Department's Assistant Secretaries for Enforcement and for Financial Institutions are co-chairing a working group of law enforcement and regulatory officials. The Action Items below represent the goals this group seeks to achieve in the coming year.

Action Item 2.3.1: **The Departments of the Treasury and Justice and the federal financial regulators will issue a joint memorandum identifying measures to improve the sharing of information between law enforcement and regulatory authorities.**

> **Lead:** Assistant Secretary for Enforcement and Assistant Secretary for Financial Institutions, Department of the Treasury.

Goal for 2000: Identify measures for the enhanced sharing of information between law enforcement and regulatory authorities.

Milestones: By the end of the year, the Departments of the Treasury and Justice, and the federal financial regulators, will issue a joint memorandum identifying measures on enhanced information sharing.

The need for enhanced and coordinated information sharing between regulatory and enforcement officials can be as great as the need for information sharing among enforcement officials themselves. Bank regulatory agencies require banks to file SARs and must continue to ensure that information uncovered during bank examinations relating to potential crimes or suspicious activity will be shared with law enforcement, where appropriate. Similarly, enforcement officials must be willing to share sensitive information with regulators so that the institutions and investors can be protected. Of course, all such information sharing must be done in such a way as to protect the confidentiality of personal data.

Complementary approaches to counter-money laundering efforts require enhanced coordination between enforcement and regulatory officials. A joint memorandum outlining steps to increase information sharing would serve as a useful model for further steps at both the federal and state levels. The joint memorandum should reflect appropriate consideration of the Ten Key Principles for the Improvement of International Cooperation Regarding Financial Crime and Regulatory Abuse endorsed by the G-7 Heads of State in June 1999. These principles are attached at Appendix 4.

Action Item 2.3.2: The Departments of the Treasury and Justice and the federal financial regulators will begin regular meetings of senior law enforcement and regulatory officials to discuss counter-money laundering efforts in each regulatory district throughout the nation.

Lead: Assistant Secretary for Enforcement and Assistant Secretary for Financial Institutions, Department of the Treasury.

Goal for 2000: Expand the number of regulatory districts where enforcement and regulatory officials meet regularly to exchange information about developing cases and discuss the possible uses of civil regulatory or criminal enforcement authority.

Milestones: By November, the Assistant Secretaries for Enforcement and for Financial Institutions, in conjunction with the Fed, will report to the Money Laundering Steering Committee on progress made in expanding the number of regulatory districts where enforcement and regulatory officials meet regularly, and discuss steps to be taken regarding any remaining regulatory districts where such meetings are not taking place.

Regular meetings between enforcement and regulatory officials are important. They can produce a valuable exchange of information about developing cases and the possible use of civil regulatory or criminal enforcement authority to deal with aspects of the money laundering problem in particular areas. Such meetings already occur in a good part of the nation, and they will be encouraged in all regulatory districts.

Action Item 2.3.3: **The Departments of the Treasury and Justice and the federal financial regulators will expand training opportunities for federal financial investigators and bank examiners.**

> **Lead**: Assistant Secretary for Enforcement and Assistant Secretary for Financial Institutions, Department of the Treasury.

> **Goal for 2000**: Conduct training of federal financial investigators and bank examiners.

> **Milestones**: By May, the Assistant Secretaries for Enforcement and for Financial Institutions will identify existing training programs for federal financial investigators and bank examiners. By the end of the year, at least two training sessions will be conducted.

Investigators need to increase their understanding of the methods and operating realities of financial institutions, and about what is and what is not practical in terms of screening or identifying transactions or customers. At the same time, regulators must understand more about the obstacles investigators face and the ways in which regulatory powers can be brought to bear to alleviate those obstacles. Enhanced training opportunities concerning counter-money laundering techniques and programs can provide a productive way to stimulate such cross-disciplinary thinking.

Objective 4:   Increase Usefulness of Reported Information to Reporting Institutions

The *1999 Strategy* recognizes that the existing reporting requirements impose costs on financial institutions, and that the government must therefore focus its reporting requirements to collect only information that is particularly useful for fighting financial crime. The *1999 Strategy* also calls for an increased public sector-private sector dialogue about the use enforcement agencies make of reported information and how the government's analysis of reported information could be made more useful not only to law enforcement, but to the financial industry itself.

> **Action Item 2.4.1: FinCEN will continue to expand the flow to banks of information based on SARs and other BSA reports, and on the utility of these reports to law enforcement.**
>
> > **Lead:** Director, FinCEN, Department of the Treasury.
> >
> > **Goal for 2000:** Enhance the amount and the quality of information based on BSA reports that is shared with the banking community.
> >
> > **Milestones**: By October, the Treasury Department will design a system to improve identification of law enforcement uses of SAR information, and will share this information with the banking community through FinCEN.

In June 1999, FinCEN began formally addressing the issue of feedback with respect to the banking, law enforcement and regulatory communities, and specifically with regard to improving mutual feedback with the banking community on SARs. Since that time, FinCEN has identified priority feedback issues in the following areas: (i) analytic feedback on money laundering trends, patterns and methodologies, (ii) utility and usage of SARs by law enforcement, and (iii) banking industry compliance. FinCEN is developing a plan and implementation strategy to address these issues, and a progress report will be provided at each regular meeting. In addition, the Treasury Department's Under Secretary for Enforcement has instructed FinCEN, the Customs Service, and the Secret Service, and requested IRS participation, to develop and implement a system to identify how SAR information is used by Treasury law enforcement. The Justice Department will contribute to this work.

Objective 5: **Work in Partnership with Associations of Legal and Financial Professionals to Ensure that Money Launderers are Denied Access to the Financial System.**

Because of the role they play as the "gatekeepers" to the domestic and international financial system, professionals -- especially lawyers, accountants and auditors -- are uniquely positioned either to facilitate money laundering or, on the other hand, to deter and detect the crime. The importance of vigorous enforcement efforts that apply to money launderers -- including corrupt professionals who design and maintain the systems through which the money launderers operate -- is addressed elsewhere in this *Strategy*. However, the legal and financial professionals whose services are used by money launderers are often not knowingly engaged in the schemes. That is, they are not corrupt professionals but instead are unwitting facilitators of money laundering schemes.

The effort to combat money laundering could be greatly enhanced if professionals take steps to ensure that they, and the businesses they serve, are not unwittingly complicit in money laundering. The government is committed to an ongoing effort to work with professionals who operate in the financial system to put systems in place to detect and prevent money laundering, and to ensure that the individuals who stand at the gate to the domestic and international financial systems have the knowledge and training to identify and assist in protecting both their institutions and the public from money laundering.

> **Action Item 2.5.1**: **A study group consisting of the Departments of the Treasury and Justice, FinCEN, the SEC, and the federal bank regulators will examine how best to utilize accountants and auditors in the detection and deterrence of money laundering.**
>
> > **Lead**: Director, FinCEN, Department of the Treasury.
> >
> > **Goal for 2000**: Heighten auditor awareness of possible money laundering and develop additional guidance, training, and educational materials that address money laundering vulnerabilities. In addition, continue to monitor various measures undertaken by the accounting profession from other countries to determine their applicability to the U.S. experience.
> >
> > **Milestones**: By September, the Director of FinCEN will report to the Money Laundering Steering Committee on progress to develop further approaches to money laundering that can be integrated into the work of both internal and external accounting professionals.

A study group was established by the Treasury Department two years ago to enhance knowledge about money laundering, encourage the issuance of guidance on money laundering vulnerabilities, and promote effective internal controls. The study group continues to improve the baseline level of knowledge among a wide assortment of accounting professionals, including management accountants, internal auditors, external auditors, and government accountants, through education and training. It has already developed and published materials for the accounting profession that highlight the risks of money laundering activity in various industries. For example, as a result of the study group's efforts, Audit Risk Alerts issued for auditors of the banking, securities brokerage, investment company, and insurance industries, included segments on money laundering. The study group will consider additional audit alerts.

Going forward, the study group will develop further approaches to money laundering that can be integrated into the work of both internal and external accounting professionals. For example, the study group is assessing how existing accounting literature, including statements on auditing standards concerning illegal acts by clients, internal controls and fraud (SAS 54, SAS 78 and SAS 82), can further its work in this area. The study group will continue its work with the AICPA, as well as with other relevant accounting organizations. In addition, the group is working with the Financial Action Task Force on Money Laundering (FATF), which recently discussed the issue at the February 2000 meeting of its Financial Services Forum.

> **Action Item 2.5.2**: **Review the professional responsibilities of lawyers and accountants with regard to money laundering and make recommendations -- ranging from enhanced professional education, standards or rules, to legislation -- as might be needed.**
>
> > **Lead**: Chief, Asset Forfeiture and Money Laundering Section, Department of Justice.
> >
> > **Goal for 2000**: Determine what, if any, enhanced professional education, standards, rules, or legislation, is needed for lawyers and accountants.
> >
> > **Milestones**: By June, an interagency working group will propose preliminary recommendations to the Money Laundering Steering Committee. These recommendations could range from enhanced education, standards, and rules to legislation. During the next few months, the working group will develop and refine the recommendations, and continue to meet with associations of lawyers and accountants. Meetings have already been held or scheduled with representatives from the American Law Institute, the American Institute of Certified Public Accountants, and the American Bar Association. Final recommendations will be issued by December.

The *2000 Strategy* remains committed to the discussion of the relationship between legitimate professional activity and unlawful participation by professionals in money laundering. As noted in the *1999 Strategy*, it is not always easy to distinguish between conduct that is criminal and conduct that amounts to either an honest effort to represent a client aggressively or to a simple failure to perform adequate due diligence. Legal rules properly insulate professional

consultations from overly broad scrutiny and create a zone of safety within which professionals can advise their clients. But those rules should not create a cover for criminal conduct.

The importance of examining this issue has recently been endorsed internationally. In October 1999, the G-8 Justice and Interior Ministers met in Moscow to discuss combating transnational organized crime. The resulting "Moscow Communique" called for, among other things, countries to consider various means to address money laundering by the professional "gatekeepers" of the international financial system, *e.g.*, lawyers, accountants, auditors, and company formation agents.

Objective 6: ***Ensure that Regulatory Efforts to Prevent Money Laundering Are Responsive to the Continuing Development of New Technologies***

> **Action Item 2.6.1: The Departments of the Treasury and Justice and the federal financial regulators will continue outreach to the private sector to ensure that anti-money laundering safeguards respond to new technologies.**
>
> > **Lead:** Director, FinCEN, Department of the Treasury.
> >
> > **Goal for 2000:** Monitor new technologies, financial services, and commercial developments -- particularly regarding the Internet and smart-cards -- and work with the private sector to encourage the implementation of anti-money laundering safeguards in new technologies.
> >
> > **Milestones:** FinCEN will continue to prepare an internal government monthly entitled "CyberNotes" which reports on significant commercial, legal or regulatory developments affecting financial services utilizing emerging technologies. Additionally, by June, FinCEN will publish for general audiences a comprehensive survey of developments affecting stored value products, Internet banking operations and Internet gaming activities.

The development of new technologies -- such as electronic cash, electronic purses, Internet- or smart-card-based electronic payment systems, and Internet banking -- is increasing the ability of individuals to rapidly transfer large sums of money, and could pose potential money laundering problems. Consequently, bank regulatory and law enforcement agencies are monitoring -- both domestically and internationally -- new legal and technological developments in these fields, and law enforcement and regulatory enforcement measures taken with respect to these businesses. In the coming year, the Departments of the Treasury and Justice and the federal financial regulators will continue this work, and will seek to expand their outreach and partnership with the private sector by meeting with developers and providers of stored value, Internet banking, and Internet casino products to identify, understand, and mitigate any problems before they arise.

> **Action Item 2.6.2: The Departments of the Treasury and Justice and the federal financial regulators will examine existing legal authorities with respect to stored value cards to determine whether current law is adequate in addressing their potential use in**

money laundering.

> **Lead:** General Counsel, Department of the Treasury.
> Chief, Asset Forfeiture and Money Laundering Section, Department of Justice.

> **Goal for 2000:** Review how current statutory and regulatory counter-money laundering authorities apply to stored value cards, and develop recommendations as to whether current law needs to be amended to address their potential use in money laundering schemes.

> **Milestones:** By November, an interagency working group will report its findings to the Money Laundering Steering Committee.

Stored value cards offer money launderers a potentially new and efficient means of transporting large sums of money in small, easily concealed cards. As the use of stored value cards becomes more prevalent, it is important to understand how this new technology fits into current statutory and regulatory schemes, and to ensure that it does not open loopholes for money launderers to exploit.

Objective 7: ***Understand Implications of Counter-Money Laundering Programs for Personal Privacy***

The *1999 Strategy* recognizes the importance of protecting the personal privacy of our citizens from unwarranted intrusions. The fight against money laundering should not -- and need not -- compromise personal privacy. Indeed, personal financial security is enhanced by safeguarding the integrity of the financial system and reducing the opportunities for abuse, manipulation, and corruption by money launderers. Following the publication of the *1999 Strategy*, a working group on privacy policy and money laundering began a detailed examination of the steps currently taken to ensure the security and confidentiality of collected BSA information This examination is intended to result in a comprehensive review of steps that might be taken to improve the protection of personal financial information without compromising the effectiveness of our anti-money laundering efforts. In addition, the President has pledged to seek new financial privacy legislation this year to go beyond the protections included in the Gramm-Leach-Bliley Act, including the provision of meaningful choice for individuals on how their information is shared within financial holding companies.

Action Item 2.7.1: The Treasury Department's working group on personal privacy and money laundering will continue its review of counter-money laundering and privacy policies, and will recommend modifications to existing counter-money laundering laws and regulations, as necessary, to enhance the protection of personal information

obtained to carry out these counter-money laundering programs.

> **Lead**: General Counsel, Department of the Treasury.
>
> **Goal for 2000:** Examine the need to enhance the protection provided to personal financial information that banks and other entities provide to the government to comply with the BSA, and that is shared among federal, state and local law enforcement agencies.
>
> **Milestones:** By May, the working group will complete its detailed description of the existing legal protections for personal information provided to the government pursuant to the BSA. The working group will then conduct thorough outreach with privacy advocates, representatives of the financial services industry, law enforcement officials, Members of Congress, and others to better understand whether the current money laundering privacy protections should be modified. By November, the working group will make recommendations to the Secretary of the Treasury for regulatory and/or legislative action, as appropriate, to enhance the protection of personal financial information.

The *1999 Strategy* established an interagency working group to conduct a 180-day review on the relationship between counter-money laundering and privacy policies. The working group has focused principally on preparing a comprehensive description of the existing privacy protections for personal financial information obtained by the government as part of its counter-money laundering efforts. The working group plans to complete its descriptive study by May and will then use its paper as the basis for an intensive study of the need for enhanced privacy protections of personal information. The working group will meet with privacy advocates, representatives of the financial services industry, law enforcement officials, Members of Congress and others interested persons to better understand whether the system for protecting the privacy of personal information collected as part of our anti-money laundering efforts should be modified. The working group will present its conclusions and recommendations, if any, for regulatory and/or legislative action to the Secretary of the Treasury by November.

Goal 3: Strengthening Partnerships With State and Local Governments to Fight Money Laundering Throughout the United States

The *1999 Strategy* identifies the growing interest and importance of state and local governments in money laundering prevention, detection, and enforcement. Increasingly, state and local governments have recognized that the illegal and often violent acts financed by money laundering are at the heart of their traditional law enforcement concerns.

Local enforcement and regulatory officials -- working with federal officials in their areas -- are well-positioned to recognize potential money laundering activity and to adjust enforcement and regulatory efforts to local conditions. For this reason, both Congress and the *1999 Strategy* called for the establishment of a federal grant program to provide seed capital for emerging state and local counter-money laundering enforcement efforts. In response, the Departments of the Treasury and Justice have made significant progress in the development of the Financial Crime-Free Communities Support Program (C-FIC). The Departments of the Treasury and Justice have executed a Memorandum of Understanding (MOU) to govern the administration of the C-FIC program, and in the upcoming year will solicit applications from eligible candidates and begin dispersing funds on a competitive basis to eligible state and local recipients. In 2000, the Departments of the Treasury and Justice will also continue to encourage state and local efforts through training, information exchange, and technical assistance. Finally, the Departments of the Treasury and Justice will conduct a campaign to reach out to state and local partners for input on the *Strategy* to ensure consistency between federal, state and local priorities and programs.

Objective 1: Provide Seed Capital for State and Local Counter-Money Laundering Enforcement Efforts

> **Action Item 3.1.1:** The Departments of the Treasury and Justice will accept applications and award grants under the C-FIC program.
>
> > **Lead:** Deputy Assistant Secretary for Enforcement Policy, Department of Treasury.
> > Director, Bureau of Justice Assistance and Office of Justice Programs, Department of Justice.
>
> > **Goals for 2000:** Award over $2.5 million in C-FIC grant funds to eligible candidates.
>
> > **Milestones:** The Treasury and Justice Departments will solicit applications and assemble peer review panels to evaluate the applications. Based on the results of this competitive application process, the Treasury Department expects to award the initial C-FIC grant monies by the end of September.

The C-FIC program was authorized by Congress in 1998, and Congress appropriated $2.9 million in fiscal year 2000 for the commencement of the program. C-FIC will provide technical assistance and training, information on best practices, and grants to support state and local law enforcement efforts to detect and prevent money laundering and related financial crimes, whether related to narcotics or other underlying offenses.

The Treasury Department, in coordination with the Justice Department, will operate the C-FIC program on a competitive basis. Location within a HIFCA will be considered a favorable factor for a C-FIC candidate, as HIFCAs are areas that have been formally designated as areas of serious money laundering concern that merit an increased focus of federal, state, and local efforts. Thus, while state and local programs within HIFCAs may be particularly appropriate grant candidates, any qualifying state or local law enforcement agency or prosecutor s office may compete for and be eligible to receive a C-FIC grant.

C-FIC grants are to be used as seed money for state and local programs that seek to address money laundering systems within their areas. Thus, for example, grant funds could be used to build or expand a financial intelligence capacity at the state or local level, or to purchase computer hardware and software for use in financial investigative analysis. Funds could also be used to train state and local law enforcement officers to detect indicia of money laundering or to train and hire auditors to monitor the money flows and recordkeeping of certain types of businesses, such as money transmitters.

C-FIC's success should not be judged simply by the amount of money it awards in grants. By making available information and analytic resources, and providing training for state and local officers, the program can reduce the need for state and local agencies to reproduce the infrastructure, or independently acquire the knowledge, necessary to investigate financial crime.
Thus, for example, a state police intelligence center could use grant funds to commission a study of cash flows or related indicia of possible money laundering in the state.

Eligibility. Any state or local law enforcement agency or prosecutor s office is eligible to receive a C-FIC grant. The applicant may propose collaborating with other agencies, but the applicant will be accountable for monitoring how all grant funds are spent.

C-FIC Contact Person for Fiscal Year 2000. The Department of the Treasury's C-FIC Coordinator for fiscal year 2000 can answer general questions about the C-FIC program and can be reached at (202) 622-0300. Questions regarding the status of specific applications should be directed to the Department of Justice Response Center at 1-800-421-6770 or (202) 307-1480. The Response Center is open Monday through Friday, 9 a.m. to 5 p.m.

Applications. The Treasury Department and BJA will develop the application package for the C-FIC program. This information will be published in an appropriate publication (such as the Federal Register) and will be posted on the BJA website (www.ojp.usdoj.gov/BJA/).

Criteria for C-FIC Grant Awards. The following criteria will be considered in the selection of the initial C-FIC grant awardees. As the C-FIC program evolves, elements of these criteria may change and additional criteria may be deemed appropriate by the Secretary of the Treasury. Material changes to the grant criteria or their weighting will be made public in accordance with applicable law.

Criterion One: Demonstration of Problem or Threat.

A grant applicant should demonstrate that it is focusing on a significant money laundering problem or risk, in a manner consistent with the *National Money Laundering Strategy.* Each application will be required to include a preliminary threat assessment that identifies the most significant money laundering risks the applicant is proposing to address using C-FIC grant funds.

Criterion Two: Inter-agency Collaboration.

A grant applicant should demonstrate how it plans to collaborate with other law enforcement agencies or prosecutor's offices to combat money laundering. For example, an application could outline how the applicant proposes to coordinate its activities with any relevant HIDTA and OCDETF efforts, and indicate whether the applicant is prepared to refer appropriate cases to these groups.

Additionally, applicants within a HIFCA should specify how they will coordinate with the HIFCA action team. State and local programs within HIFCAs are particularly appropriate grant candidates, and will receive some preference in the award process.

Criterion Three: Focus on Money Laundering as Such.

C-FIC grants should help state and local law enforcement officials and prosecutors understand, investigate, disrupt, and prosecute those involved in money laundering systems. The grants should not be used to fund investigative efforts focused primarily on the predicate crimes that generate launderable proceeds.

Criterion Four: Effectiveness and Performance Measures.

Each applicant should submit an analysis of how it will target the problem that it seeks to address, and how it will measure its success. Effectiveness need not be measured in terms of immediate arrests or cash seizures, although such statistics may be relevant.

Criterion Five: Lasting Effect.

C-FIC applicants should describe how the use of the C-FIC award funds can result in progress being made against money laundering activity that will continue after the grant award period has expired.

Criterion Six: Collaboration with Regulators and Experts.

Applicants should demonstrate how the design and contemplated operation of their programs invites participation by relevant regulatory officials and integrates knowledge from appropriate academic or research disciplines.

Criterion Seven: Monitoring Expenditures.

Applicants will be required to describe how they will monitor grant expenditures. The description should include statements of the experience of the applicable managers in overseeing program funds.

Criterion Eight: Proposed Budget.

Each application will be required to include a proposed budget showing in detail how any award will be used.

Grant Awards and Conditions. C-FIC grant awards will be made by the Secretary of the Treasury, in consultation with the Attorney General. In general, a C-FIC award in fiscal year 2000 will not exceed $300,000.[9]

Accountability. Each successful applicant will be required to establish a system to measure and report the results of the use of the grant funds. The reporting system should include biennial surveys to measure progress and effectiveness. As part of its reporting obligations, the grant recipient will also be required to assess the level of cooperation between it and the federal, state, and local law enforcement agencies and regulators involved in fighting money laundering and related financial crimes.

Administration of the C-FIC Program. The Treasury Department, in consultation with the Justice Department, will set C-FIC program policies and oversee the selection of grant awardees. BJA and the Office of Justice Programs (OJP) will administer the C-FIC program pursuant to their MOU with the Department of the Treasury. BJA and OJP will disburse the grant funds and maintain and operate all necessary data and reporting systems for grant applications and disbursements, and oversee the audit of grant awardees.

Objective 2:   Promote the Free Flow of Relevant Information Between State and Federal

---

[9] Federal law requires that any recipient of a C-FIC grant agree to return C-FIC monies awarded to the extent that monies are received by the grantee via asset forfeiture as a result of efforts funded by the grant. 31 U.S.C. 5352(c)(1).

Enforcement Efforts

The *1999 Strategy* identifies FinCEN's Gateway Program as a key tool for enhancing the access of state and local law enforcement to the valuable BSA information maintained by the federal government. The Action Item in this section represents our continued commitment to expanding the Gateway Program, and ensuring that state and local law enforcement have the maximum appropriate access to the information they need to fight money laundering.

> **Action Item 3.2.1:** **The Departments of the Treasury and Justice will reach out to state and local authorities broadly for contributions to the *National Money Laundering Strategy*, to ensure that federal priorities are consistent with and complementary to state and local strategies.**
>
> > **Lead:** Assistant Secretary for Enforcement, Department of the Treasury.
> > Assistant Attorney General, Criminal Division, Department of Justice.
> >
> > **Goal for 2000:** Solicit input on the *National Money Laundering Strategy* from state and local regulatory and enforcement agencies.
> >
> > **Milestones:** The Department of the Treasury and Justice will reach out to state and local officials to discuss the *National Money Laundering Strategy*. By November, the Assistant Secretary and Assistant Attorney General will report to the Money Laundering Steering Committee the results of the outreach.

Expanded state and local participation in the development of the *Strategy* is required for it to be truly "national." To date, though there have been consultations, there has been no systematic outreach to state and local authorities. In the coming year, the Departments of the Treasury and Justice will institute an outreach effort to ensure that the contribution of state and local money laundering authorities to the *Strategy* is maximized.

> **Action Item 3.2.2**: **The Department of the Treasury will promote the use of FinCEN's Gateway Program as a vehicle for two-way information exchange and joint state-federal financial analysis projects**.
>
> > **Lead**: Director, FinCEN, Department of the Treasury.
> >
> > **Goal for 2000:** Enhance the current Gateway access processes by developing and implementing a new memorandum of understanding between FinCEN and appropriate state officials. Additionally, begin the transition of current Gateway users to the new Secure Web System, institutionalize the training program, and sponsor a State Coordinators Conference.

Milestones: By June, FinCEN, in concert with state representatives from New Jersey, will establish a new training program and process that will be used to enhance the utility of the data made available via Gateway. In addition, the FinCEN Office of Chief Counsel will complete the MOU between FinCEN and Gateway users. During the Summer, FinCEN will host the State Coordinators Conference.

Federal, state, and local law enforcement officials are beginning to realize the importance of following the money and in particular utilizing the financial data available through FinCEN. The Gateway program originally permitted a central coordinator in each state to access FinCEN databases. However, demand for access to Gateway data has vastly increased, both among state and federal law enforcement. Bringing the state and federal users together under Gateway affords the investigators the opportunity not only to get direct, online access to FinCEN data, but also to be networked with other federal, state and local authorities through an "alert" program. In September 1999, FinCEN hosted a meeting with state law enforcement and regulatory representatives to assess their needs, and it was determined that Gateway users sought a secure web system for data access and communication. FinCEN has acted upon this need, and the preliminary technological links between FinCEN and the IRS Detroit Computing Center that will allow for secure data access and retrieval, consistent with proper confidentiality practices, have been installed and are being tested.

Objective 3:   Encourage Comprehensive State Counter-Money Laundering and Related Legislation

> **Action Item 3.3.1**: **The Departments of the Treasury and Justice will provide technical assistance for enhanced state laws against money laundering.**
>
> > **Lead**: Assistant Attorney General, Criminal Division, Department of Justice.
> >
> > **Goal for 2000**: Convey to state authorities the federal government's interest in helping states to enhance laws against money laundering, and respond to requests from state authorities seeking assistance.
> >
> > **Milestones**: By June, the Justice Department will issue a letter to governors encouraging reviews and enhancements, where necessary, of state anti-money laundering laws. By November, the Assistant Attorney General will report to the Money Laundering Steering Committee on the extent of assistance required and on plans to meet this need.

At last count, seventeen states have still not made money laundering a state crime, and some state laws against money laundering have serious gaps to cover. These weaknesses should be speedily closed. State money laundering statutes are essential if states are to be full partners in the national counter-money laundering effort, and the federal government will make its resources available to facilitate that partnership.

The Department of Justice will issue a letter to the governors of the fifty states encouraging them to review their state's laws against money laundering and offering assistance in enhancing state anti-money laundering statutes. To facilitate this review, experts at the Departments of the Treasury and Justice will assist states that are considering enacting or revising statutes dealing with money laundering or financial reporting and recordkeeping. Assistance can take the form of producing information about the patterns of money laundering encountered in a state, or providing drafting or related advice about the terms of the necessary statutes themselves or related legal issues. The Administration also will encourage states to enact legislation licensing and regulating appropriate money services businesses and those engaged in the business of transporting currency.

Objective 4: Support Enhanced Training for State and Local Investigators and Prosecutors

> **Action Item 3.4.1: The Departments of the Treasury and Justice will complete revision of a model curriculum for a financial investigations course for state and local law enforcement agencies, hold "Train the Trainer" national conferences, and distribute the curriculum.**
>
> > **Lead:** Assistant Attorney General, Criminal Division, Department of Justice.
> >
> > **Goal for 2000:** Revise and distribute a model curriculum.
> >
> > **Milestones:** By June, the Department of Justice will finalize and distribute the new curriculum.

Training in financial investigations is no less essential for state and local enforcement professionals than for their federal counterparts. Indeed, organizations such as the National Association of Attorneys General and the National District Attorneys Association have in the past produced some of the most comprehensive money laundering training and resource materials available. To help meet the needs of state and local law enforcement agencies for up to date training materials, a new investigations training curriculum will be distributed in the summer of 2000 which includes Training Coordinator Guides, Instructor Guides, and Participant Guides, as well as supplementary graphic presentations and videos.

Goal 4: Strengthening International Cooperation to Disrupt the Global Flow of Illicit Money

Financial crime havens and underground financial markets around the world are a critical part of a global system for hiding criminally earned profits. For this reason, efforts to counter international financial crime have been placed squarely on the national security agendas of the United States and its allies. The *1999 Strategy* articulated an aggressive international agenda designed to improve international cooperation through diplomatic efforts, policy development, regulatory oversight, practical enforcement, and the provision of training and technical assistance. The United States has been and will continue working closely with its international partners in bilateral and in the multilateral contexts to effect positive change in the area of money laundering.

A number of important steps have been taken since the *1999 Strategy* was released. Interagency working groups have reviewed correspondent banking relationships with certain types of institutions, and outlined a concrete agenda to involve the international financial institutions more actively in the fight against money laundering. At the same time, the FATF has made significant progress by welcoming new observer members, fostering the creation of regional sister organizations, and beginning the process of identifying non-cooperative jurisdictions. Negotiations toward a United Nations Convention against Transnational Organized Crime continue to show promise. The G-8 justice ministers issued an important communique covering financial crime issues. And practical law enforcement and regulatory cooperation continues, but with an intensified sense of urgency, in the face of the explosion of globalized financial services.

In many important respects, this year's *Strategy* is a continuation of last year's efforts. But this year promises to be auspicious in its own right. FATF is expected to issue a report on non-cooperative jurisdictions, the OECD will issue a report on its Harmful Tax Competition project, and the Financial Stability Forum is expected to issue a report that will address, among other things, the effects of offshore financial centers on global financial stability. Thus, we will have a unique opportunity to explore the nature of the ties between the distinct but related realms of money laundering, taxation, and prudential oversight of financial institutions. Real progress can be made in policy discussions to articulate these connections and to persuade the international community of the need for continuing cooperation among officials involved in these various activities.

Even more important, events over the past five months have demonstrated the need for new legislation to deal with international money laundering issues. As described in Action Item 4.1.1, the Treasury Department needs additional tools to ensure that appropriate steps can be taken with respect to money laundering havens. And these tools are needed now, so that the United States can respond effectively to emerging threats, and participate actively in multilateral fora. Several Members of Congress have proposed legislation on these issues as well. We look forward to working closely with interested Members to pass a strong bill this year.

Objective 1: **Seek Legislation Enhancing the Government's Ability to Protect U.S. Institutions and the U.S. Financial System from International Money Laundering.**

The United States already has powerful statutory tools to combat money laundering. Loopholes and missing pieces, however, remain in our counter-money laundering structure. In the next year, the Administration will be supporting at least two bills to enhance our ability to combat money laundering – one would give the Secretary of the Treasury powerful new authority to protect the U.S. financial system from international money laundering and financial crime havens, and the other would provide law enforcement with enhanced weapons to combat money laundering at home and abroad.

> **Action Item 4.1.1:** **The Administration will seek enactment of the International Counter-Money Laundering Act of 2000.**
>
> > **Lead:** Assistant Secretary for Legislative Affairs, Department of the Treasury.
> >
> > **Goal for 2000:** Enactment of the International Counter-Money Laundering Act of 2000.

The authority of the Secretary of the Treasury to protect the U.S. financial system from being abused by money launderers operating through international financial crime havens is not as robust as it could be. Currently, there is a broad gap between two tools currently available -- informational advisories to U.S. banks about specific jurisdictions or transactions, which encourage additional scrutiny, and International Emergency Economic Powers Act (IEEPA) sanctions, which block transactions with designated entities in a jurisdiction. New gap-filling authorities are needed to give the Secretary the discretion to take targeted, narrowly tailored and proportional action against those jurisdictions, foreign financial institutions, or types of transactions that pose particular money laundering threats. These new discretionary authorities will allow the Secretary -- in consultation with the Secretary of State, the Attorney General and the Federal Reserve -- to address jurisdictions, financial institutions, and/or types of transactions that are of primary money laundering concern to the United States by:

- Requiring U.S. financial institutions to maintain records and/or report on aggregate transactions, or each transaction, with such a jurisdiction or institution, or regarding such a transaction;

- Requiring U.S. financial institutions to ascertain the real-party-in-interest of accounts opened or maintained in the U.S. by a foreign person (except for publicly traded foreign corporations or trusts) involving such a jurisdiction, institution or transaction;

- Requiring U.S. financial institutions to ascertain the identities of persons who are permitted to use such an institution's payable-through or correspondent account with a U.S. financial institution;

- Prohibiting or imposing conditions on U.S. financial institutions' correspondent accounts with such a financial institution or foreign jurisdiction.

Objective 2: *Apply increasing pressure on jurisdictions where lax controls invite money laundering.*

A consensus has developed over recent years -- both within the United States and throughout the world -- that financial crime havens pose an international threat that must be addressed. However, agreeing on the relevant factors for evaluating countries, and then applying these factors has proven to be a difficult and complex task. The year 2000 has the potential to be a watershed year, as it will mark the culmination of numerous identification and evaluation processes, both multilaterally and within the United States. Consequently, 2000 will present the opportunity for significant international action against financial crime havens.

Significant international action, however, will require more than simply evaluation and identification. Once financial crime havens have been identified, appropriate countermeasures must be implemented. In this regard, the United States prefers to take multilateral action in support of multilateral determinations, though we reserve the right to act unilaterally when necessary to protect our financial system or other national interests. Unfortunately, the United States has only limited tools to employ against financial crime havens, and therefore the Administration has requested that Congress enact the International Counter-Money Laundering Act of 2000 in order to provide it with a full range of countermeasures. (See Action Item 4.1.1). In any case, the United States will assemble all the tools available to it, and take appropriate action in response to the threat posed by financial crime havens.

This Objective is divided into two broad Action Items, which are in turn broken down into Sub-Action Items. The first Action Item discusses ongoing efforts to identify financial crime havens, beginning with U.S. efforts and proceeding on to multilateral efforts. The second Action Item discusses potential countermeasures that can be taken against identified havens, this time beginning with preferred multilateral action and proceeding on potential U.S. unilateral action.

Action Item 4.2.1: Identify jurisdictions that pose a money laundering threat to the United States.

Sub-Action Item 4.2.1.a: The United States will complete an internal evaluation of financial crime havens.

Lead: Under Secretary for Enforcement, Department of the Treasury.

Goal for 2000: Implement a new methodology to evaluate and categorize jurisdictions into groups of increasing concern, based on the nature of the jurisdiction's financial crime problem and the degree to which it has taken constructive steps -- or is willing to take such steps -- to address the problem.

Milestones: By May, the interagency working group formed to conduct the 90-day review of correspondent banking relationships will identify priority jurisdictions for U.S. attention, and outline specific strategies with respect to each of them. The working group will report to the Money Laundering Steering Committee on results and actions taken.

The *1999 Strategy* called for the formation of an interagency working group to explore whether measures should be adopted to restrict financial institutions in the United States from opening or maintaining correspondent banking accounts for foreign banks that are organized in jurisdictions in which they do not offer banking services to residents and which are not subject to adequate supervision by home country authorities. The examination of correspondent banking will continue as discussed in Action Item 4.7.3. However, the Money Laundering Steering Committee has directed the working group to identify havens and money laundering threats to the United States.

The working group has devised a process that will measure countries against the following factors:

•   Does the jurisdiction have a money laundering problem that the United States considers important? This determination takes into account the findings made in the money laundering section of the State Department's annual International Narcotics Control Strategy Report (INCSR).

•   Is the jurisdiction primarily a source of criminal funds, or is it primarily a destination/transit point for such funds? This distinction is intended to facilitate targeted application of different countermeasures to different types of problems. (See Action Item 4.2.2 for further discussion).

•   Does the jurisdiction have an adequate anti-money laundering regime? This determination will be based on the jurisdiction's laws and implementation, including law enforcement and regulatory cooperation with the U.S., with specific reference to the FATF 40 Recommendations (See Appendix 2), and the FATF 25 criteria for determining non-cooperative countries and territories (See Appendix 3).

•   If the jurisdiction does not have an adequate anti-money laundering regime, are its laws and/or its implementation of anti-money laundering laws being improved?

•   If the jurisdiction's laws and/or implementation of laws are not improving, is this primarily due to a lack of political will, or is it reasonable to expect an improvement during the period under review?

•   In addition, the analysis will take into account the interplay between tax evasion -- a serious crime in its own right -- and money laundering. It is clear that many of the same factors that make a jurisdiction attractive as a tax haven make it attractive as a money laundering haven.

Sub-Action Item 4.2.1.b: Support the on-going efforts of FATF to identify non-cooperative jurisdictions based upon its twenty-five criteria.

> **Lead:** Under Secretary for Enforcement, Department of the Treasury.

> **Goal for 2000:** Completion by June of the FATF Ad Hoc Group on Non-Cooperative Countries or Territories (NCCTs) project to identify, review, and name non-cooperative jurisdictions.

> **Milestones:** By May, the U.S. will participate in multilateral groups that will research and analyze the laws, regulations and practices of jurisdictions thought by FATF members to be potentially non-cooperative. A report is to be completed on each of the high priority jurisdictions and submitted to the June 2000 FATF Plenary, where it is expected that FATF will identify and name specific non-cooperative jurisdictions. In October, FATF will begin a second round of analysis.

Over the past year, FATF's Ad Hoc Group on NCCTs has finalized its criteria for identifying non-cooperative jurisdictions, and has now begun the actual evaluation process in direct consultations with the jurisdictions in question.[10] The United States will actively participate in this process by serving on regional review groups that will apply the FATF criteria to individual jurisdictions. Once this process is complete in June, FATF will announce the jurisdiction labeled as non-cooperative, and begin to consider appropriate countermeasures.

> **Sub-Action Item 4.2.1.c: Support efforts of the Financial Stability Forum (FSF) and regional fora in urging countries and jurisdictions to adopt and adhere to international anti-money laundering standards.**

> > **Lead:** Senior Deputy Assistant Secretary, International Monetary and Financial Policy, Office of International Affairs, Department of the Treasury.

> > **Goal for 2000:** Finalize work of the FSF to develop procedures for assessing the compliance of Offshore Financial Centers (OFCs) with international standards on financial regulation and supervision, and the exchange of information.

---

[10] The criteria are included at Appendix 3. FATF papers describing the criteria and the process used by FATF to review particular jurisdictions are posted on FATF's website at www.oecd.org/fatf/pdf/NCCT-en.pdf.

Milestones: By April, the OFC Working Group's conclusions will be reported to the FSF.

The FSF, created pursuant to a G-7 initiative in April 1999, set up an OFC working group comprised of officials of industrial and emerging market economies, international organizations, and international regulatory and supervisory groupings to review the role of OFCs in the international financial system. The working group's work plan is focused on encouraging OFCs to adopt and implement international regulatory standards. The working group is developing recommendations on mechanisms for assessing compliance in the implementation of the standards, and ensuring appropriate incentives to enhance such compliance. The working group's efforts also take into account the FATF 40 Recommendations (see, Appendix 2) and the G-7 Ten Key Principles on Information Exchange for the Improvement of International Cooperation Regarding Financial Crime and Regulatory Abuse (see, Appendix 4), which include standards relevant to financial fraud and money laundering. The United States is actively participating in the FSF, and will work to ensure that its efforts are consistent and coordinated with other relevant international efforts.

In complementary efforts, the Committee on Hemispheric Financial Issues (CHFI) and the Asia Pacific Economic Cooperation (APEC) have provided political impetus to enhance financial regulation and supervision in their regions. Their statements have specifically referred to anti-money laundering initiatives.

Sub-Action Item 4.2.1.d: Support multilateral efforts to identify tax havens.

Lead: Assistant Secretary for Tax Policy, Department of the Treasury.

Goal for 2000: Publication by the OECD of a list of jurisdictions classified as "tax havens" under the criteria established by the OECD, and a rapid and successful conclusion of the OECD's work on bank secrecy.

Milestones: The U.S. and its OECD colleagues have completed a technical review of jurisdictions that may be classified as tax havens under the criteria provided for in the OECD Report on Harmful Tax Competition, and a list of "tax havens" is expected to be published after receiving approval from the OECD Council in June. The Committee on Fiscal Affairs is currently considering a report on access to bank information for tax purposes. The U.S. will remain an active participant in the discussions on this report. The Committee is expected to make a final decision on the report in March.

Although tax evasion and money laundering are distinct crimes, they share many common characteristics, including the use of practices designed to conceal financial assets and transactions from the appropriate government authorities. Money launderers are often guilty of tax fraud or other fiscal crimes, and they will generally seek to avoid scrutiny of their activities by tax authorities to minimize their risk of prosecution for tax evasion. Moreover, many of the features that make a jurisdiction attractive as a tax haven -- *e.g.* excessive bank secrecy, lack of transparency, and a lack of effective exchange of information -- are precisely the features that attract money launderers. Thus, many potential countermeasures are applicable to both. Indeed, with respect to countries that are both tax and money laundering havens, coordination of countermeasures may enhance effectiveness in both areas.

<u>Action Item 4.2.2</u>: Take appropriate action with respect to identified financial crime havens.

As noted above, the U.S. will take appropriate action against financial crime havens in support of the multilateral efforts discussed in Action Item 4.2.1, while reserving the right to act unilaterally when necessary. However, before discussing countermeasures, it is necessary to understand the different types of international financial crime threats to the United States. Generally, these threats can be categorized as follows:

- Developed economic and financial centers by their very nature afford criminals the opportunity to engage in money laundering on a large scale, and therefore in this sense pose money laundering "threats" to the United States. However, for the most part, economically and financially developed countries are committed to ongoing processes to combat money laundering. These countries are our allies in the fight against international money laundering, and the only appropriate action for us to take with respect to these countries is continued cooperation.

- Many jurisdictions struggle with domestic crime and corruption problems that make them a source of illegally earned proceeds that are laundered throughout the world, including in the United States. These jurisdictions often face continuing problems of political will and capacity in dealing with what are, at root, domestic problems of crime and corruption. They can be characterized as "source" jurisdictions for criminal proceeds that are laundered internationally, though are often not "destination" jurisdictions where the proceeds are actually laundered and sheltered. These jurisdictions must address their underlying problems of crime and corruption, in addition to instituting effective counter-money laundering regimes.

- Many jurisdictions neither adequately participate in international efforts to combat money laundering and financial crime nor generate significant criminal proceeds as a result of domestic crime and corruption. Rather, these jurisdictions tend to be characterized by underregulated offshore financial services and excessive bank secrecy, and thus they act as financial crime havens by intentionally attracting the proceeds of crime committed elsewhere. Such jurisdictions have either deliberately not embraced international efforts to combat financial crime or have irresponsibly undertaken steps to diversify their economies without putting in place the necessary regulatory safeguards.

Mindful of these considerations, the U.S. will seek to employ the fullest range of available

63

countermeasures, each appropriately targeted to the specific jurisdiction and circumstance in question.

Sub-Action Item 4.2.2.a: The U.S. will take appropriate action in support of multilateral efforts.

Lead: Deputy Secretary, Department of the Treasury.

Goal for 2000: Implement countermeasures in support of and coordination with FATF, the FSF, and the OECD Harmful Tax Competition initiative, as well as FATF regional-style bodies.

Milestones: The United States will review the results of the FATF, the FSF, and the OECD initiatives and will support their efforts to implement coordinated countermeasures. By its September plenary, FATF should have discussed a plan to implement appropriate countermeasures with respect to non-cooperative jurisdictions.

By the July G-7 economic summit in Okinawa, FATF, the FSF, and the OECD will all have released reports and begun the process of identifying possible countermeasures. At the summit and within the respective multilateral efforts, the Treasury Department, in close consultation with the Departments of State and Justice, will support the application of strong multilateral countermeasures to identified jurisdictions. In particular, the United States will advocate within FATF and other international fora that a broad range of appropriate countermeasures be identified and applied.

Sub-Action Item 4.2.2.b: Promote adoption of supervisory and regulatory actions -- such as increased regulatory reporting, increased external and internal audits, differentiated risk treatment -- in response to specified jurisdictions that fail to make progress in implementing effective international standards relating to money laundering.

Lead: Senior Deputy Assistant Secretary for International Monetary and Financial Policy, Office of International Affairs, Department of the Treasury.

Goal for 2000: Increase focus on and discussion of further actions that can be taken by supervisory authorities with respect to identified problem jurisdictions.

Milestones: As appropriate and as part of the bank regulation and supervision process, bank regulatory agencies will consider additional supervisory and regulatory remedies for operations or exposure of U.S. banks in specified jurisdictions.

In November and December 1999, an interagency subgroup convened to work on several action items relating to international financial issues, including supervisory and regulatory actions. After extensive review of the application of differentiated risk-weights on bank lending to entities in offshore jurisdictions, various members of the subgroup noted that offshore lending has generally not been a source of primary concern within the regulatory community. Lending generally represents a smaller portion of offshore affiliate business, when compared to other types of activities pursued offshore; and since much of this lending may be interbank or with affiliates in non-offshore jurisdiction, the risk-weighting framework would not apply. Deposit activities, trust and private banking programs, insurance and reinsurance are activities not covered by the risk weighting framework of the Basel Capital Accord. Unilateral imposition by the US of such risk weighting rules would have significant competitive implications for US financial institutions vis-à-vis other Basel member institutions operating offshore.

Overall, the Treasury Department and the U.S. financial supervisory authorities continue to strongly advocate efforts in various international fora to encourage offshore centers to strengthen financial supervision and prudential supervision. We continue to work in multilateral bodies such as the Basel Committee on Banking Supervision to promote the concept of additional supervisory actions that can be taken when banking supervisors encounter difficulties in obtaining information needed for supervision of their institutions across borders, including within offshore jurisdictions. Appropriate supervisory actions will be considered and the various sets of incentives being developed by the international financial community will be reviewed. The U.S. banking supervisory authorities will continue to play an active role in these initiatives.

Sub-Action Item 4.2.2.c: Issue bank advisories when appropriate.

> **Lead**: Under Secretary for Enforcement, Department of the Treasury.

> **Goal for 2000**: Identify jurisdictions with inadequate counter-money laundering regimes that should be targeted with the issuance of bank advisories.

> **Milestones**: By July, the United States will identify countries that are the potential subject of advisories.

Pursuant to its authority under the BSA, the Treasury Department may issue bank advisories to U.S. financial institutions. These advisories -- which are issued only after close consultation with the Departments of State and Justice -- inform U.S. financial institutions of significant U.S. government concern regarding particular classes of transactions, and recommend that financial institutions give enhanced scrutiny to such transactions. For example, in April 1999, after negotiation failed to produce meaningful improvement in the counter-money laundering regime of Antigua and Barbuda, the Treasury Department issued an advisory alerting U.S. financial institutions to give enhanced scrutiny to all financial transactions routed into or out of that country. The advisory prompted Antigua and Barbuda to implement improvements to its financial supervisory regime.

As our experience with Antigua and Barbuda demonstrates, advisories are a valuable tool with respect to foreign jurisdictions with inadequate counter-money laundering regimes. Preferably, they can be issued in support of multilateral determinations or initiatives, but they can also be issued unilaterally in order to safeguard U.S. financial institutions. As discussed in Action Item 4.2.1, in the coming year the United States will be involved in both multilateral and unilateral efforts to identify money laundering havens, and the issuance of advisories will often be an appropriate response to countries so identified.

> **Sub-Action Item 4.2.2.d:** **Implement the Foreign Narcotics Kingpin Designation Act and consider using IEEPA powers to target narcotics-related money launderers in other appropriate circumstances.**

> > **Lead:** Director, Office of Foreign Assets Control, Department of the Treasury.

> > **Goal for 2000:** Implement the Foreign Narcotics Kingpin Designation Act ("Kingpin Act") against significant foreign narcotics traffickers and their organizations and operatives worldwide and, where appropriate, continue to consider invoking the powers of IEEPA.

> > **Milestones:** By June 1, 2000, and every June 1 thereafter, the Kingpin Act requires the President to report to Congress those foreign persons that are determined to be significant foreign narcotics traffickers appropriate for sanctions and to impose the Kingpin Act's IEEPA-like sanctions against them.

The U.S. now has at its disposal two powerful economic sanctions tools against significant foreign narcotics traffickers, the entities they own or control, and those persons acting for them or supporting their narcotics trafficking activities. In addition to IEEPA, which is a weapon that the President has used for the past five years against Colombian drug cartels, the U.S. also will now use the new Foreign Narcotics Kingpin Designation Act against significant foreign narcotics traffickers on a global basis. Both the Kingpin Act and IEEPA prohibit U.S. persons from engaging in transactions, trade and services involving foreign narcotics kingpins and derivative designees.

The Kingpin Act was signed into law on December 3, 1999. Following the approach being used against Colombian drug cartels under IEEPA, the Kingpin Act is directed at significant foreign narcotics traffickers and their organizations and operatives throughout the world but is not aimed at foreign countries. The Kingpin Act requires that the Departments of Treasury, Justice, State and Defense, and the CIA coordinate to develop a list of recommended kingpins for presidential designation by June 1 each year. Despite the annual June 1 deadline, the statute provides for kingpin designations at other times as well. Therefore, the coordination and designation process will be ongoing permanently throughout the year.

The long-term effectiveness of the Kingpin Act, as well as of any IEEPA program, will depend heavily on the Treasury Department's authority to make derivative designations of entities and individuals.

The predicate for the Kingpin Act was the imposition in 1995 of IEEPA sanctions against narcotics traffickers centered in Colombia. This is a powerful on-going program against Colombian drug cartels. As required by PDD-42, IEEPA sanctions have been employed to bar U.S. persons from having any trade or financial transactions with individuals and businesses owned or controlled by or acting for significant foreign narcotics traffickers centered in Colombia (Executive Order 12978, October 21, 1995). In addition, the Order blocks the assets of such individuals and businesses subject to U.S. jurisdiction. These actions not only prevent U.S. persons from being unwitting aiders and abettors, and potential victims, of narcotics traffickers, but also protect the integrity of our financial institutions and deny criminals the ability to operate as legitimate businesses.

Objective 3: ***Continue to Work with Countries to Adopt and Adhere to International Money Laundering Standards***

United States international counter-money laundering efforts are not limited to taking action against non-cooperative jurisdictions. Indeed, to promote international cooperation, the U.S. will continue to support the articulation, universal implementation, and where appropriate, enhancement of international money laundering standards. This support takes the form both of active participation in the development and implementation of these standards and in assistance to jurisdictions seeking to bring themselves into compliance.

> **Action Item 4.3.1: Work toward universal implementation of the FATF 40 Recommendations.**
>
> > **Lead:** Under Secretary for Enforcement, Department of the Treasury.
> >
> > **Goal for 2000:** The United States will maintain its leadership role in the FATF and existing FATF-style regional bodies. It will seek expansion of membership to additional appropriate governments, and support FATF outreach efforts to encourage implementation of the FATF 40 Recommendations by non-member jurisdictions.

Milestones: An interagency working group will analyze available information on potential candidates for FATF membership and determine -- in advance of the June meeting of the FATF -- appropriate nominations to be made based on FATF criteria for new membership. New FATF observer members -- Argentina, Brazil, and Mexico -- will complete the necessary steps to meet all the requirements to become full members of FATF by the end of the year. The U.S. will encourage the FATF to (i) complete the first round of mutual evaluations of Gulf Cooperation Council states by the end of the year, and (ii) conduct at least three high level missions or seminars to raise awareness and encourage expanded implementation of the 40 Recommendations by non-members.

More than ten years after its creation, the FATF remains the premier multilateral body devoted to countering money laundering. Membership of the FATF comprises 26 industrialized nations and two regional organizations.[11] A major component of the FATF's work involves ongoing peer review of each member's national counter-money laundering measures by one another, based on the FATF 40 Recommendations. (See Appendix 2). Members of the FATF have made significant advances in articulating the measures necessary to combat money laundering effectively, as outlined in the 40 Recommendations, and in implementing those measures domestically.

The FATF is extending its message. One aspect of this effort is expansion of the FATF's membership. Last year, the FATF welcomed Argentina, Brazil, and Mexico as observers and, this year, it will conduct a peer review of those countries' money laundering controls. The Gulf Cooperation Council (GCC) is a member of FATF, although GCC member states are not. Last year, for the first time, five GCC member states (Bahrain, Kuwait, Oman, Qatar, and United Arab Emirates) agreed to undergo FATF-style mutual evaluations. These evaluations are anticipated to be completed during 2000.

Action Item 4.3.2: Promote the development of FATF-style regional bodies.

Lead: Under Secretary for Enforcement, Department of the Treasury.

Goal for 2000: Consolidation of recently created FATF-style regional bodies, and establishment of such bodies where they do not yet exist, such as in South America.

Milestones: The United States will encourage the Asia Pacific Group on Money Laundering (APG) to develop a mutual evaluation program by the end of the year. The U.S. will continue to provide qualified examiners to mutual evaluation programs of the

---

[11] Originally, the FATF consisted of 15 members, and the European Commission. Currently, the member countries of the FATF are: Australia, Austria, Belgium, Canada, Denmark, Finland, France, Germany, Greece, Hong Kong (China), Iceland, Ireland, Italy, Japan, Luxembourg, the Netherlands, New Zealand, Norway, Portugal, Singapore, Spain, Sweden, Switzerland, Turkey, the United Kingdom, and the United States. The European Union and the Gulf Cooperation Council are also members.

other regional bodies, as well as the Offshore Group of Banking Supervisors (OGBS). The U.S. will encourage the two newly created FATF-style bodies in Africa to become operational by the end of the year. The U.S. will encourage Argentina and Brazil to establish a FATF-style body in South America also by the end of the year.

FATF-style regional bodies -- which endorse the 40 Recommendations and have established a process of mutual evaluation -- already exist in the Caribbean and part of Latin America, as well as in Central and Eastern Europe. In addition, the OGBS, though not a regional body, has endorsed the FATF 40 Recommendations (see Appendix 2) and has embarked upon a process of peer review to assess its members' implementation of these standards.

Several other regional counter-money laundering groups have been established and are in varying stages of development. Last year at its annual meeting, the APG agreed in principle to establish a mutual evaluation process for its members based on the FATF 40 Recommendations. These developments are encouraging, although overall progress has been slow. In Africa, two new regional anti-money laundering bodies were established last year. In November 1999, representatives of seven nations signed the Eastern and Southern Africa Anti-Money Laundering Group's Memorandum of Understanding[12]. In December 1999, the Groupe Intergouvernemental D'Action Contre le Blanchiment de L'Argent en Afrique was officially formed by 15 countries of Western Africa, from Mauritania to Nigeria. And most recently, the Finance Ministers of Argentina and Brazil have pledged to create a FATF-style body in South America. However, none of these groups has yet become operational.

Additionally, in early 1999, the Organization of American States (OAS) adopted the *Commitment of Mar del Plata*, which prescribes numerous OAS and FATF endorsed anti-money laundering measures designed to assist OAS member states in impeding the financing of terrorist organizations.

> **Action Item 4.3.3**: **Negotiate strong anti-money laundering provisions in the pending United Nations Convention against Transnational Organized Crime.**
>
> > **Lead:** Assistant Secretary, Bureau for International Narcotics and Law Enforcement Affairs, Department of State.

---

[12] The signatories to the MOU included Malawi, Mauritius, Mozambique, Namibia, Seychelles, Tanzania, and Uganda.

Goal for 2000: Inclusion of strong anti-money laundering provisions within the Convention, including a requirement for governments to criminalize non-drug-related money laundering and to institute comprehensive anti-money laundering regulatory regimes.

Milestones: The U.S. seeks to complete negotiations of the Convention by the end of the year.

The United Nations has not concluded a convention that addresses money laundering since the 1988 Vienna Convention. The Vienna Convention requires signatories to criminalize drug money laundering, but does not address regulatory controls. The current negotiation of a Convention against Transnational Organized Crime presents an opportunity for the international community to require nations to criminalize the laundering of proceeds of serious, organized crime and to adopt a range of regulatory measures to protect financial institutions from abuse by launderers. The United States will continue to seek anti-money laundering provisions that will maintain the integrity of the existing international standards. Successful conclusion of the Convention, with a specific commitment by all State Parties to develop anti-money laundering regulatory and supervisory regimes based on the FATF 40 Recommendations (see Appendix 2), would represent an important advance in the effort to ensure global adoption and implementation of comprehensive money laundering controls.

Action Item 4.3.4: **The United States will continue to urge the international financial institutions (IFIs) to explore mechanisms to encourage and support countries, in the context of financial sector reform programs, to adopt anti-money laundering policies and measures.**

Lead: Senior Deputy Assistant Secretary, International Monetary and Financial Policy, Office of International Affairs, Department of the Treasury.

Goal for 2000: Include assessment of adherence to money laundering standards where appropriate as a more routine part of financial sector reform programs, assessments, and reviews, and include anti-money laundering issues in IFI training and technical assistance programs. Focus G-7 discussion of anti-money laundering efforts by IFIs. Follow through on the U.S. request that the IMF, working together with the other IFIs, study the magnitude of money laundering and its macroeconomic impact, analyzing in particular the effects of money laundering flows on various economies.

Milestones: The United States will discuss with IFIs policy, program design and assessment, as well as enhanced potential engagement, relating to technical assistance focused on anti-money laundering.

The IMF, the World Bank, and the regional development banks are increasingly sensitive to the problems of international money laundering. In recent years they have provided structural reform assistance to help selected countries strengthen their banking supervisory capacity, improve corporate governance and transparency, and adopt financial sector reforms. In 1999, the United States and the IFIs shared views on anti-money laundering policies, programs and progress. The United States supports proposals to further engage the IFIs in efforts to deter money laundering as part of the multilateral effort. In addition, the United States will discuss with our G-7 partner countries how best the IFIs might promote the adoption of anti-money laundering measures in the context of financial sector program design and assistance, where appropriate (i.e., in those cases where money laundering is identified as a particular vulnerability or risk). The United States will convey the importance of multilateral and bilateral, as well as individual country, anti-money laundering measures at the Economic Summits, the meetings of G-7 Finance Ministers and Central Bank Governors, and the annual meetings of the IMF and World Bank.

Many of the IFIs have extensive technical assistance programs in the area of financial sector reforms in bank supervision and regulation, legal and commercial law, and other financial system infrastructure. Discussion with the IMF and World Bank have indicated their willingness to work with the US (and other member countries) to identify how to better focus on money laundering in the context of financial sector reform programs.

> ### Action Item 4.3.5: Enhance the provision of training and assistance to nations making efforts to implement counter-money laundering measures.
>
> > **Lead:** Assistant Secretary, Bureau for International Narcotics and Law Enforcement Affairs, Department of State.
> >
> > **Goals for 2000:** Provide a comprehensive and coordinated program of training and technical assistance to countries seeking to implement comprehensive internationally-recognized money laundering counter-measures. Expand the use of multilateral organizations and International Law Enforcement Academies (ILEAs).
> >
> > **Milestones:** At the September annual meeting of international organizations and donor countries involved in providing such assistance, U.S. representatives will share information about our ongoing programs, and take into consideration information received from other participants in formulating the coming year's priorities. Additionally, by November, the Assistant Secretary will report to the Money Laundering Steering Committee on the status of international money laundering training and assistance.

The United States is committed to offering training and technical assistance to nations seeking to implement comprehensive internationally-recognized money laundering controls. Programs of the Departments of State, Justice, the Treasury, and the federal financial regulators all provide such assistance. These efforts must continue to be supported if they are to succeed.

The State Department coordinates requests from U.S. embassies and other sources for a variety of training, including law enforcement, financial services supervision and prosecutorial training as they relate to anti-money laundering programs. These requests are coordinated with the agencies responsible for delivering assistance and with other donor states and international organizations. During 1999, the United States funded over 70 financial crime and money laundering courses and seminars in 40 countries. We will endeavor to ensure that resources are appropriately allocated and coordinated through the various international organizations through which the United States provides much of its international training.

Additionally, the U.S. this year intends to create a training curriculum for countries facing the problem of international terrorist financing. This curriculum -- targeted to foreign investigators, prosecutors and judges -- will be based on existing anti-money laundering training programs, but will concentrate specifically on terrorist financing.

> **Action Item 4.3.6: Support and expand membership of the Egmont Group of financial intelligence units.**
>
> **Lead:** Director, FinCEN, Department of the Treasury.
>
> **Goal for 2000:** Expanded membership and participation in the Egmont Group.
>
> **Milestones:** FinCEN expects to assist four new units to become operational by the end of 2000. FinCEN will reach out to new Egmont Group members and eleven priority countries to encourage the introduction of anti-money laundering legislation, and support the development of financial intelligence units in these countries. FinCEN will expand by ten percent the number of investigative information exchanges via the financial intelligence unit network consistent with the Egmont Group principles. FinCEN will complete upgrades of the Egmont Secure Website to further support information exchanges and other communications between and among FIU members of the Egmont Group.

One of the most important developments in the implementation of international counter-money laundering standards has been the successful cooperation between and among financial intelligence units (FIUs). These agencies are created to receive their own domestic suspicious activity reports (required under their respective internal laws), analyze financial information related to law enforcement activity, disseminate information to domestic enforcement agencies, and exchange information internationally.

Currently, 48 financial intelligence units participate in the Egmont Group. As an active participant, FinCEN coordinated a total of 217 information exchanges in 1999. It is imperative to encourage the continued and expanded use of this network for case development and investigations by domestic law enforcement. FIUs can play a critical role in ongoing investigations and in the effective implementation of anti-money laundering measures. The U.S. law enforcement community should take every opportunity to exploit the information available from other FIUs to support U.S. investigations.

Objective 4:   Advance the International Fight Against Corruption.

The proceeds of corruption must, like other ill-gotten gains, be laundered if they are to be secured and enjoyed. Moreover, money laundering itself represents a corrupting influence on financial systems and institutions. Over the past several years, the U.S. has been involved in a number of initiatives aimed at stemming the tide of corruption, including the negotiation of the OECD's convention against commercial bribery of foreign public officials, the Inter-American Convention Against Corruption, the Group of Nations Against Corruption (GRECO) of the Council of Europe, the U.N. Ad Hoc Committee which is negotiating anti-money laundering articles in the U.N. Transnational Organized Crime Convention, and a growing number of global and regional anticorruption actions. There has been considerable progress made in the fight against corruption, most notably through the Vice-President's First Global Forum on Fighting Corruption which was held in Washington last year. The Second Global Forum will be co-hosted by the Netherlands and the United States, and is scheduled for May, 2001. U.S. involvement on a range of international efforts is expected to deepen and grow.

The Action Items listed below addressing corruption are designed to complement the efforts already underway in the United States.

> **Action Item 4.4.1: Expand the list of money laundering predicates under U.S. law to include numerous foreign crimes, including public corruption, not currently covered by the money laundering statute.**
>
> > **Lead:** Assistant Attorney General, Office of Legislative Affairs, Department of Justice.
>
> > **Goal for 2000:** Enact legislation the Money Laundering Act of 2000.

As noted in Action Item 1.3.1, the Administration seeks enactment of the the Money Laundering Act of 2000, which seeks to enhance the ability of law enforcement to investigate and prosecute money laundering. This legislation includes an important tool to the fight against corruption. Loopholes now exist in our money laundering statutes that would allow foreign public officials accepting bribes to use U.S. banks to launder proceeds. The new provision will close that loophole, which severely limits the ability of the United States to investigate and prosecute the laundering of the proceeds of foreign corruption through financial institutions in the United States.

> **Action Item 4.4.2: Urge other nations to make public corruption a predicate offense under their own anti-money laundering statutes.**
>
> > **Lead:** Under Secretary for Enforcement, Department of the Treasury.
> > Assistant Secretary for International Narcotics and Law Enforcement,

Department of State.

Assistant Attorney General, Criminal Division, Department of Justice.

Goal for 2000: Increase the number of countries that have public corruption as a predicate offense in their anti-money laundering statutes.

Milestones: The United States will push to include on the agenda of the next FATF presidency the study of bribery as a predicate offense, and will raise the issue in other international negotiations related to corruption.

As part of the battle against public corruption, the international community has begun to address the importance of money laundering controls to the effective implementation of anti-corruption measures. For example, an OECD working group has reported that it considers bribery a serious offense for the purposes of money laundering legislation and has asked the FATF to review the issue with its membership. The United States will work to ensure that this issue is addressed by the FATF within the next Presidency.

An OAS working group on probity and public ethics has also begun to consider measures to enhance the effectiveness of the Inter-American Convention Against Corruption, which the United States signed in 1996 and which is now awaiting Senate ratification. Provisions to criminalize public acts of corruption in the context of organized crime are being negotiated in the U.N. Convention Against Transnational Organized Crime. Additionally, the U.S. participated in the Council of Europe's Criminal Law Convention on Corruption, which provides that parties make corruption offenses predicates for their anti-money laundering statutes. The United States will seek to ensure that current or future international negotiations involving public corruption will provisions for governments to make public corruption offenses money laundering predicates.

Action Item 4.4.3: The Treasury Department, working in cooperation with the Departments of State and Justice, will coordinate an interagency effort to examine the problem of foreign government officials who make use of the international financial system to convert public assets to their personal use.

Lead: Assistant Secretary for International Affairs, Department of the Treasury.

Goal for 2000: Enhance our understanding of the impact on national economies of large-scale official corruption and of existing legal authorities that can be used to address this issue. Using this knowledge, devise appropriate policy initiatives to combat this activity.

Milestones: In March, the Assistant Secretary of the Treasury for International Affairs will coordinate an interagency Foreign Official Corruption Working Group to address this issue, in coordination with and drawing in part on the findings of the subgroup discussed below. The Working Group will devise appropriate policy initiatives, and report its preliminary results to the Money Laundering Steering Committee in June.

Corrupt government officials who systematically divert public assets to their personal use undermine U.S. efforts to promote durable democratic political institutions and stable, vibrant economies abroad. The destabilizing impact can be particularly great, and the vulnerability of government institutions to corrupt officials' activities, can be especially substantial, in countries with emerging democratic systems and developing or transitional economies. Often, corrupt officials rely on international money laundering to assist the clandestine diversion of public assets.

The Assistant Secretary of the Treasury for International Affairs, in cooperation and coordination with the Departments of Justice and State, will coordinate the Working Group to devise appropriate policy initiatives. This effort will be based in part on the findings of the subgroup described below that will be convened in March.

> **Sub-Action Item 4.4.3.a: The Departments of the Treasury, State, and Justice will review the tools and methodologies available to identify, trace and seize stolen assets of other countries (in particular how the international financial system is used to launder these assets) and make recommendations, as necessary, for enhancements or additional authorities.**
>
> > **Lead:** Assistant Attorney General, Department of Justice
> > General Counsel, Department of the Treasury.
> > Legal Adviser, Department of State.
> >
> > **Goal for 2000:** Enhance our understanding of the available legal authorities and investigative tools that can be used in this area, and develop recommendations, as necessary, for enhancements or additional authorities.
> >
> > **Milestones:** By June, the subgroup will report its findings to the Foreign Official Corruption Working Group.

In order to develop appropriate policy initiatives in this complex area, it is necessary first for a thorough analysis be completed of existing relevant legal authorities and options, and of potential avenues for enhancement.

Objective 5:   *Develop and Support Additional Multilateral Efforts to Facilitate Information Sharing.*

Action Item 4.5.1: **Urge the G-7 nations to consider an initiative to harmonize rules relating to international funds transfers so that the originators of the transfers will be identified.**

> **Lead:**   Director, Division of Bank Operations and Payment Systems, Federal Reserve Board.
> Under Secretary for Enforcement, Department of the Treasury.

> **Goal for 2000:**   Include in a report from the G-7 Finance Ministers to the Heads of State a recommendation to harmonize the rules to identify the originators of international funds transfers within the G-7 and for the G-7 to encourage other nations to do the same.

> **Milestones:**   In February, the U.S. presented to an informal working group of G-7 delegates to the FATF, a paper on the harmonization of rules regarding international funds transfers. This paper will be discussed by the group and sent to the G-7 Deputies to be incorporated into a final report from the Finance Ministers to the Heads by the Okinawa Summit.

Each G-7 country should have rules that require international funds transfer messages to include the identity of the originator. Harmonized rules of this sort would add great effect to each jurisdiction's own rules on funds transfers and would limit further the ability to dodge detection through cross-border funds transfers. Such a step is essential to permit effective detection of international money laundering activities.

To facilitate the harmonization of these rules, G-7 countries should engage their financial institutions in a dialogue about steps needed to ensure that their record-keeping requirements take account of and allow for legitimate concerns regarding privacy, commerce, and the security of information being provided. That dialogue must be deepened and intensified. As payments systems of all types are developing ever more rapidly, and as a premium is increasingly placed on the efficiency and speed of payments systems, these developments ought not to provide a respite from the need by all financial institutions to be vigilant toward those who would attempt to secrete funds derived from illegal sources.

Action Item 4.5.2: **Expand law enforcement information exchange and judicial cooperation channels.**

> **Lead:**   Legal Advisor, Department of State.
> Assistant Attorney General, Criminal Division, Department of Justice.

Goal for 2000: Create new mutual legal assistance treaties (MLATs), tax information exchange agreements, and other sharing agreements. Work to expand financial regulators' ability to use MLATs for law enforcement purposes.

Milestones: Conduct a mid-year review of progress in creating new agreements.

The Departments of the Treasury, Justice, and State will continue to identify priority countries where MLATs, extradition treaties, or FIU memoranda of understanding concerning information exchange should be negotiated or enhanced to support money laundering investigations, prosecutions, and forfeitures. During the summer of 2000, the Departments of the Treasury, Justice, and State will review progress in creating new mutual legal assistance treaties, tax information exchange agreements, and other sharing agreements. These agreements are essential components of money laundering investigations, prosecutions, and forfeitures.

U.S. financial regulators can in certain countries use existing MLATs between the U.S. and foreign governments to obtain evidence for use in their investigations and enforcement actions. In certain instances, however, financial regulators are not able to use an existing MLAT, either because the language of the agreement does not contemplate use other than by criminal authorities or, because the agreement is narrowly interpreted by the foreign authority. Work to expand financial regulators' use of MLATs will also be pursued.

Additionally, tax administrators around the world are recognizing the need to obtain greater access to information with respect to accounts and activities of taxpayers in foreign jurisdictions. This is relevant to money laundering, as it is often the case that the same bank secrecy regimes that safeguard tax evaders also serve to safeguard money launderers. Consequently, the extent to which a jurisdiction becomes less attractive as a tax haven will often make it less attractive as a money laundering haven. For several years, the Treasury Department has had a firm policy of refusing to enter into new tax treaty relationships with countries that are unwilling to engage in information exchange. As a result of this policy, the United States has succeeded in convincing some countries to modify their laws and practices to allow U.S. tax authorities access to financial information, even though such countries had not previously engaged in information exchange with other countries on tax matters.

> **Action Item 4.5.3:** **Create an interagency team from FinCEN, the Federal Reserve Board, Treasury, Justice and other appropriate agencies, to promote understanding of mechanisms and processes associated with the movement of criminal proceeds into, through and out of the United States and among other at-risk nations.**
>
> **Lead:** Director, FinCEN, Department of the Treasury.
>
> **Goal for 2000:** Implement a multilateral framework to encourage the study and exchange of information about illicit currency movements based on joint analyses of

available financial transaction data and investigative information.

> **Milestones:** By September, the interagency team will develop an action plan. By the end of the year, the various members of the interagency team will seek to implement the action plan through various international fora.

FinCEN will lead an interagency effort to create an action plan to develop information about illicit currency movements using existing information exchange arrangements. The action plan will be keyed to research and analysis based both on SAR reporting and ongoing or after-action money laundering investigative activity. The interagency team will then coordinate outreach to the international community. Examples could include FinCEN outreach to the Egmont Group, Fed outreach among appropriate Central Bank authorities, Treasury Department outreach in FATF, and Justice Department outreach among appropriate liaison channels such as Interpol. Every effort will be made to achieve actual exchange of relevant information beginning in 2001. FinCEN will be responsible for building a model or models of illicit currency flows based in part or entirely on the resulting information as soon as sufficient data has been collected.

Objective 6:   Improve Coordination and Effectiveness of International Enforcement Efforts.

> **Action Item 4.6.1:** **The Departments of the Treasury, State, and Justice will work together to enhance information sharing on known or suspected alien money launderers to facilitate the denial or revocation of visas held by such persons.**

> > **Lead:** Assistant Attorney General, Criminal Division, Department of Justice.

> > **Goal for 2000:** Increased information exchange to ensure that the names of known or suspected money launderers are entered into the visa lookout system, and the establishment of a centralized process for collecting and passing of future names. Additionally, the Administration will seek new legislation enabling the State Department to deny or revoke visas held by aliens engaged in money laundering.

> > **Milestones:** By the end of the first quarter of 2000, the Departments of Justice and State will implement an agreement on the modalities for passing to the State Department names and biographic data of known or suspected money launderers to ensure that the names are entered into the visa lookout system.

Money laundering is a national security threat. Under existing law, aliens who knowingly engage in the laundering of drug proceeds are ineligible for United States visas. To assist in the enforcement of these visa laws, law enforcement agencies regularly share information on drug traffickers and drug money launderers with State Department consular offices abroad, both through existing information exchange systems and on an ad hoc basis. In late 1999, the Departments of Justice and State held preliminary meetings to enhance information sharing on drug money launderers. These efforts will lead to additional entries in relevant lookout systems to help ensure that such individuals do not obtain U.S. visas. Moreover, new proposed legislation would further enable consular officers to deny or revoke the visas of money launderers, regardless of whether the laundering involved drug proceeds.

Objective 7:   Build Knowledge and Understanding

There are a great many issues concerning money laundering and its broader economic effects about which we need much better knowledge.

> **Action Item 4.7.1**: **Continue to advance the work on estimating the magnitude of money laundering.**
>
> > **Lead**: Director, FinCEN, Department of the Treasury.
> >
> > **Goal for 2000**: Award a contract to one or more firms to develop a methodology for estimating the magnitude of money laundering. The methodology will address both domestic U.S. and international aspects of the magnitude of money laundering. Additionally, continue to work with the international community to address long-term problems associated with global criminal proceeds data collection, harmonization and money laundering modeling.
> >
> > **Milestones**: A contract for development of a methodology will be awarded by July. Also by July, FinCEN, in its capacity as chair of the FATF Ad Hoc Working Group on Estimating the Magnitude of Money Laundering, will continue to coordinate FATF efforts to develop an estimate of drug money laundering in FATF member nations.

Because money laundering by its nature defies detection, it is extremely difficult to measure progress in this area without being able to quantify with some degree of precision the amount of money laundering (and the proceeds of crime that are laundered). Existing estimates -- such as that referred to in the background section of this document -- unfortunately lack a strong scientific basis. In order to meet the long-standing concerns of the Congress and the Office of Management and Budget, FinCEN has taken a leading role in the related efforts to measure both the domestic and international magnitude of money laundering. Internationally, FinCEN has chaired the FATF Ad Hoc Working Group on Estimating the Magnitude of Money Laundering since 1998. Domestically, in fiscal year 1999 and fiscal year 2000 a total of $1 million was allocated for FinCEN to develop a methodology for estimating the magnitude of U.S. domestic money laundering. An additional $500,000 is included in FinCEN's fiscal year 2001 budget request.

During fiscal year 1999, FinCEN organized and chaired two interagency committees -- Economic Policy and Law Enforcement -- to identify available data and recommend a strategy for estimating the magnitude of money laundering. Because of the lack of useful data on the proceeds of crimes other than drug trafficking, the committees recommended that a private contractor be engaged to propose a methodology to address the data issue as well as to produce a magnitude estimate. The process of identifying a private firm capable of delivering a useful estimate began in August 1999, with final selection to be completed by July.

Action Item 4.7.2: The Departments of the Treasury and Justice, and the federal financial regulators, will assess the implications for money laundering of the increasing availability through the Internet of financial services offered to U.S. persons by foreign financial service providers.

Lead: Chief, Asset Forfeiture and Money Laundering Section, Department of Justice.

Goal for 2000: Assess the scope of the money laundering problem related to the enhanced access through the Internet of U.S. persons to offshore financial services providers.

Milestones: The Departments of Justice will lead an interagency study group that will examine how offshore financial institutions are using the Internet to offer money laundering services, and the extent to which this practice has facilitated money laundering by persons in the United States. By December, the study group will report its findings to the Money Laundering Steering Committee.

The explosive growth of the Internet over the last decade, and especially its use as the principal vehicle for e-commerce, has given rise to a number of public policy issues. Among these issues is the use of the Internet by certain offshore financial service providers to offer money laundering services to persons within the United States. Soliciting comments and perspective from law enforcement, regulators, the banking and financial services industry as well as e-commerce corporations and entrepreneurs will offer a sense of the actual extent of the problem. This will provide a basis for developing an appropriate policy that addresses the problem without inhibiting the demonstrated benefits and further commercial potential of the Internet.

Action Item 4.7.3: Continue to examine the nature of correspondent banking accounts and other international financial mechanisms, such as payable through accounts, private banking, and wire transfers, and determine the nature and extent of their susceptibility to abuse by money launderers.

> **Lead:** Under Secretary for Enforcement, Department of the Treasury.

> **Goal for 2000:** To have an enhanced understanding of correspondent banking accounts and other international financial mechanisms (such as payable through accounts, wire transfers, private banking, and trade in precious metals) and how they can be abused by money launderers, and to consider steps that could be taken to reduce such abuse.

> **Milestones:** By July, a study group (previously the 90 Day Working Group on Correspondent Banking) will consult with private sector representatives to discuss correspondent bank accounts and other international financial mechanisms.

Correspondent banking relationships and other international financial mechanisms such as payable through accounts, private banking, and wire transfers are important features of the international banking system. But these mechanisms are also potential vehicles for money laundering. They should continued to be examined, and ways of addressing potential abuses without unduly disrupting legitimate economic activity should be identified.

Appendix 1: Federal Money Laundering Laws and Enforcement

I.   Money Laundering Laws and Regulations

The two principal legal foundations for the federal government's current counter-money laundering efforts are the Money Laundering Control Act of 1986[13] and the Bank Secrecy Act of 1970,[14] along with the regulations issued by the Secretary of the Treasury to implement these laws.

Money Laundering Control Act

In 1986, Congress enacted the Money Laundering Control Act (MLCA), which established money laundering as an independent federal offense, punishable by prison sentences of up to 20 years. The intent of the MLCA is:

> [t]o create a Federal offense against money laundering; to authorize forfeiture of the profits earned by launderers; to encourage financial institutions to come forward with information about money launderers without fear of civil liability; to provide Federal law enforcement agencies with additional tools to investigate money laundering; and to enhance the penalties under existing law in order to further deter the growth of money laundering.[15]

The provisions of the MLCA criminalizing money laundering are codified at 18 U.S.C. 1956 and 1957.

Section 1956

Section 1956 includes three different types of money laundering offenses.

Section 1956(a)(1). This subsection makes it unlawful to knowingly engage in a financial transaction with the proceeds of a specified unlawful activity[16] under the following four circumstances:

- *Intent to promote specified unlawful activity.* Section 1956(a)(1)(A)(i) prohibits conducting a

---

[13] Pub. L. 99-570, Title I, Subtitle H, Sections 1351-67, 100 Stat. 3207-18 through 3207-39 (1986).

[14] Pub. L. 91-508, Titles I and II, 84 Stat. 1114 (1970).

[15] S. Rep. No. 433, 99th Cong., 2d Sess. 1 (1986).

[16] The term "specified unlawful activity" includes a broad range of criminal offenses, including narcotics trafficking, fraud, violent crimes, terrorism, and other offenses typical of organized crime. These predicate offenses are listed at 18 U.S.C. 1956(c)(7).

financial transaction involving illegal proceeds with the intent to promote specified unlawful activity. Such transactions include the reinvestment of the proceeds of crime into a criminal organization.

- *Intent to violate certain tax laws.* Section 1956(a)(1)(A)(ii) prohibits conducting a financial transaction involving illegal proceeds with the intent to engage in conduct constituting a violation of sections 7201 or 7206 of the Internal Revenue Code.[17]

- *Concealment of criminal proceeds.* Section 1956(a)(1)(B)(i) makes it an offense to conduct a financial transaction "knowing that the transaction was designed in whole or in part . . . to conceal or disguise the nature, the location, the source, the ownership, or the control of the proceeds of specified unlawful activity." This prong of the statute addresses activity that is most commonly associated with money laundering, for example, using drug proceeds to purchase stock in the name of a third party, or purchasing and mistitling automobiles to conceal the fact that the true owner of the vehicle is a drug dealer.

- *Avoidance of Reporting Requirements.* Section 1956(a)(1)(B)(ii) makes it an offense to conduct a financial transaction in order to avoid a state or federal reporting requirement. For example, such conduct would include intentionally structuring bank deposits in numerous $9,000 increments in order to avoid the BSA's requirement that banks report currency transactions of more than $10,000.

Section 1956(a)(2). This subsection involves the international movement of illicit proceeds into, out of, or through the United States. It makes it unlawful to transport, transmit, or transfer a monetary instrument or funds into or out of the United States:

- with the intent to promote the carrying on of specified unlawful activity; or

- where the defendant knows that the funds represent the proceeds of some form of unlawful activity and that the transportation or transfer is designed to conceal or disguise the nature, location, source, ownership, or control of the proceeds of specified unlawful activity or to avoid a transaction reporting requirement.

Section 1956(a)(3). This subsection enables law enforcement to conduct undercover "sting" operations. It makes it unlawful to engage in a financial transaction with property represented to be proceeds of specified unlawful activity. The funds in section 1956(a)(3) cases are not actually derived from a real crime; they are funds provided to money launderers by undercover law enforcement agents.

---

[17] Under Section 7201, the willful attempt to defeat of evade tax payments is a felony. Section 7206 makes false and fraudulent statements in tax returns and related documents a felony.

84

Section 1957

This section makes it unlawful to knowingly conduct a monetary transaction in criminally derived property in an amount greater than $10,000, which, in fact constitutes proceeds of a specified unlawful activity. Such monetary transactions must be conducted by, through, or to a financial institution. However, for the purposes of this section, financial institutions include not only banks, but also other entities such as currency exchangers, securities brokers, insurance companies, dealers in precious metals, real estate brokers, casinos, and car, boat, or airplane dealers. In other words, this section makes it unlawful in many circumstances to spend large sums of known criminal proceeds.[18]

Bank Secrecy Act

Congress enacted the BSA to counteract the use of financial institutions by criminals to launder the proceeds of their illicit activity.[19] It authorizes the Secretary of the Treasury to issue regulations requiring financial institutions to keep certain records and file certain reports, and to implement anti-money laundering programs and compliance procedures. The title of the Act is misleading, as the BSA's main purpose is to limit, rather than to enhance, secrecy regarding certain financial transactions. A willful violation of the BSA may result in a criminal fine of up to $500,000 or a ten-year term of imprisonment, or both. A violation of the BSA also may result in a civil penalties.

Two major statutes amending the BSA were enacted during the 1990s.

- The Annunzio-Wylie Money Laundering Act added several significant provisions to the BSA.[20] The most important of those provisions for the first time authorized the Secretary of the Treasury to require bank and non-bank financial institutions to report suspicious transactions.[21] It also allowed for the promulgation of rules requiring anti-money laundering programs at financial institutions, added a BSA civil penalty for negligence, and created a BSA Advisory Group of government and private-sector experts. Annunzio-Wylie also amended the MLCA to make the

---

[18] There are three important distinctions between section 1957 and section 1956. First, section 1957 has a $10,000 threshold requirement for each transaction. There is no threshold requirement for section 1956. Second, section 1957 simply requires that a monetary transaction occur with proceeds known to be of criminal origin. Unlike section 1956, there is no requirement that the transaction occur with the intent to promote a specified unlawful activity or to conceal the origin of the proceeds. Third, unlike section 1956, section 1957 requires that the transaction be conducted through a financial institution.

[19] See n. 14.

[20] Pub. L. 102-550, Title XV of the Housing and Community Development Act of 1992, 106 Stat. 3672, 4044-4074 (1992).

[21] Federal bank supervisory agencies had been requiring financial institutions to report suspicious transactions to law enforcement and regulatory authorities since 1985.

operation of an illegal money transmitting businesses a crime (this provision is codified at 18 U.S.C. 1960), and added provisions to the federal banking laws that required agencies to consider the revocation of the charter of any depository institution convicted of money laundering.

- The Money Laundering Suppression Act (MLSA) expanded upon the policies set forth in Annunzio-Wylie.[22] The most noteworthy provisions of the MLSA required the designation of a single agency as the recipient of Suspicious Activity Reports, expanded the authority to require the reporting of cross-border transportation of certain negotiable instruments, and required registration with the Treasury Department of certain non-bank financial institutions, such as money transmitters and check-cashiers.

Suspicious activity reporting requirements

Beginning in 1985, the federal bank supervisory agencies required financial institutions that they supervised to report actual or potential violations of law and suspicious transactions to federal law enforcement authorities and the supervisory agencies on what was then referred to as the Criminal Referral. In 1987, after Congress criminalized money laundering, the bank supervisory agencies added a requirement that financial institutions report known or suspected instances of money laundering and know or suspected violations of the BSA. In 1996, as the result of a desire by the bank supervisory agencies to simplify the process of reporting suspicious transactions, a new Suspicious Activity Report system was initiated that allowed all reporting entities to use the same form and submit the form to one location. Moreover, as the result of legislation authorizing the Secretary of the Treasury to require the reporting of suspicious activity by bank and non-bank financial institutions, the Treasury Department, through FinCEN, became a participant in the SAR program and also took on the responsibility of being the database manager for the SAR system. Each of the banking agencies and FinCEN issued new or revised regulations to conform the regulatory requirements with the new SAR form. To avoid confusion for financial institution filers, the agencies have made it clear that completing a SAR in accordance with the SAR instructions will constitute compliance with all of the agencies suspicious activity reporting requirements, including those contained within the Bank Secrecy Act (31 CFR 103.21).

BSA reporting requirements

The BSA authorizes the Secretary of the Treasury to promulgate rules requiring financial institutions to file certain reports of financial transactions. Financial institutions covered by these rules must file suspicious activity reports, currency transaction reports, reports of cross-border currency transportation, and reports relating to foreign bank and securities accounts. Compliance by banks with the regulators' reporting requirements constitutes compliance with the suspicious activity reporting required by the BSA

---

[22] Pub. L. 103-325, Title IV of the Riegle Community Development and Regulatory Improvement Act of 1994 (1994).

regulations.

Banks are required to file, in accordance with 31 CFR 103.21, reports of suspicious transactions conducted or attempted at their branches, and involving or aggregating to at least $5,000. A bank must file a Suspicious Activity Report (SAR) if it knows, suspects, or has reason to suspect that a transaction or series of transactions involves illegally-derived funds, is designed to evade BSA requirements, or has no business or apparent lawful purpose. Banks are specifically prohibited from notifying any person involved in a transaction reported as suspicious that a SAR has been filed. Banks enjoy a safe harbor from civil liability for any disclosure contained in a SAR.

The currency transaction reporting rules at 31 CFR 103.22 require a financial institution[23] to file a currency transaction report (CTR) for each deposit, withdrawal, currency exchange, or other payment or transfer conducted by or through the financial institution in an amount exceeding $10,000.[24] This requirement also applies to casinos, which must file reports of currency transactions involving more than $10,000, as well as the Postal Service which must file reports of cash purchases of postal money orders and other money services products worth more than $10,000. Multiple transactions occurring in a single business day must be aggregated for purposes of reaching the $10,000 threshold if the financial institution knows that the transactions are conducted by or on behalf of the same person. In accordance with exemption procedures issued by the Secretary of the Treasury, banks may exempt transactions with certain customers from the requirement to file a CTR.

A CMIR must be filed, in accordance with 31 CFR 103.23, by all persons physically transporting currency or monetary instruments in amounts exceeding $10,000 across the U.S. border, and by all persons receiving a cross-border shipment of currency or monetary instruments in excess of $10,000 for which a CMIR has not been filed. Failure to file such a report can lead to seizure of the funds attempted

---

[23] Under the BSA, the Secretary of the Treasury has the authority to define the term "financial institution" very broadly. At present, however, the implementing regulations restrict the scope of this term (for purposes of the BSA) to mean each agent, agency, branch, or office within the United States of any person doing business as a bank, a broker or dealer in securities, a money services business (defined to include a check-casher, a currency exchanger, an issuer, seller, or redeemer of travelers' checks, money orders or stored value, a money transmitter, and the U.S. Postal Service), a telegraph company, a casino, a card club, and a person subject to supervision by any state or federal bank supervisory authority.

[24] The Secretary of the Treasury may, pursuant to 31 CFR 103.26, lower an applicable reporting or recordkeeping dollar threshold when issuing a geographic targeting order (GTO). To issue a GTO, the Secretary must determine that reasonable grounds exist for concluding that additional recordkeeping and reporting requirements are necessary to carry out the purposes and prevent evasions of the BSA. A GTO may be issued with regard to a specific financial institution or group of financial institutions within a geographic area.

to be transported.

A foreign bank account report (FBAR) must be filed, in accordance with 31 CFR 103.24, by U.S. residents and citizens, as well as persons in and doing business in the U.S., regarding accounts maintained with foreign banks or securities brokers or dealers. Such reports must be filed with the Commissioner of the Internal Revenue Service for each year during which the foreign account is maintained.

BSA recordkeeping requirements

The BSA also authorizes the Secretary of the Treasury to promulgate rules requiring financial institutions to maintain certain records pertaining to financial transactions. In some instances, records must be maintained in conjunction with the filing of a report. There are additional recordkeeping requirements not attached to the duty to file a report. Examples of such independent recordkeeping requirements include the monetary instrument identification or "log" requirement and the funds transfer rules, described below. Financial institutions must keep a copy of required records for five years, and the copy must be filed or stored in such a way as to be accessible within a reasonable time, in accordance with 31 CFR 103.38.

The log requirement, found at 31 CFR 103.29, requires financial institutions to maintain records of the sale of bank checks or drafts, cashiers' checks, money orders, and travelers' checks purchased with currency in amounts of $3,000 - $10,000, inclusive. In complying with this requirement, financial institutions must obtain and record identifying information with respect to the purchaser and the instrument purchased.

Financial institutions must keep records with respect to most classes of customer transactions. One important class of recordkeeping requirements relates to funds transfers of $3,000 or more, as provided by 31 CFR 103.33. The exact nature of the funds transfer recordkeeping requirement varies depending upon the role the financial institution plays in the transaction stream, but generally requires financial institutions to maintain a copy of the payment order, payment instructions received, and, in certain circumstances, information relating to the originator, beneficiary, and intervening financial institutions.

II.   Money Laundering Enforcement and Compliance

The responsibility for enforcing our criminal money laundering laws, and ensuring compliance with the BSA's recordkeeping and reporting requirements, is shared among several federal agencies.

Law Enforcement

The Department of the Treasury and the Department of Justice are the key federal agencies responsible for enforcing the criminal prohibitions of money laundering found in 18 U.S.C. 1956 & 1957.

The Department of the Treasury

The Secretary of the Treasury, through the Under Secretary (Enforcement), oversees the money laundering enforcement efforts of the Treasury. Treasury bureaus involved in enforcing the counter-money laundering laws include the Financial Crimes Enforcement Network (FinCEN), Internal Revenue Service-Criminal Investigative Division (IRS-CI), the United States Customs Service (Customs), the United States Secret Service (USSS), and the Bureau of Alcohol, Tobacco and Firearms (ATF).

- FinCEN establishes, oversees and implements policies to prevent and detect money laundering. FinCEN links law enforcement, financial and regulatory communities into a single information-sharing network. Using BSA information reported by banks and other financial institutions, FinCEN serves as the nation's central clearinghouse for broad-based intelligence and information sharing on money laundering that helps illuminate the financial trail for investigators to follow as they track criminals and their assets. FinCEN also provides tactical intelligence and analytic support to law enforcement. It combines information reported under the BSA with other government and public information that is provided to the law enforcement community in the form of intelligence reports. These reports assist law enforcement in building investigations and planning new strategies to combat money laundering.

- The IRS-CI investigates criminal and civil money laundering and currency reporting violations under the criminal and financial codes of Titles 18 and 31, and has primary investigative jurisdiction for money laundering crimes involving banks and other financial institutions. It shares investigative jurisdiction with several other federal law enforcement agencies of criminal money laundering violations. This authority is often shared with the federal law enforcement agency with the investigative authority over the predicate crime, if such crime is outside the investigative jurisdiction of IRS-CI.

- Customs' primary anti-money laundering role is to conduct illegal drug and currency interdiction at U.S. borders. Customs also enforces the reporting of currency and monetary instruments brought into or removed from the United States, as required by the BSA. Customs has a broad grant of authority to conduct international financial crime and money laundering investigations and initiatives within its role as a border enforcement agency. This jurisdiction is triggered by the illegal movement of criminal funds, services, or merchandise across national borders. Customs enforcement efforts focus on international criminal organizations whose corrupt influence often affect trade, economic, and financial systems on a global basis. In addition, Customs operates the Money Laundering Coordination Center, which serves as a depository for all intelligence information gathered through undercover money laundering investigations and functions as the coordination and deconfliction center for both domestic and international undercover money laundering operations.

- The Secret Service and ATF both investigate money laundering cases as part of their traditional law enforcement functions. The jurisdiction of the Secret Service includes computer crimes, counterfeiting and many crimes involving the misuse of national banks and federally chartered thrift institutions.

The Department of Justice

The Attorney General, as the chief law enforcement officer of the United States, is responsible for the enforcement of all federal law. Through the Deputy Attorney General and the Assistant Attorney General for the Criminal Division, and in conjunction with the 94 United States' Attorneys, the Attorney General oversees prosecutions for money laundering offenses. The Asset Forfeiture and Money Laundering section (AFMLS) of the Criminal Division, the Special Operations Division (SOD), and the Federal Bureau of Investigation (FBI) and the Drug Enforcement Agency (DEA) are the principal Justice Department components engaged in the investigation and prosecution of money laundering.

- AFMLS is the Department of Justice's focal point for money laundering and asset forfeiture matters. The Section devises and implements DOJ policy initiatives in the domestic and international arenas with particular emphasis in the work of the Financial Action Task Force and related matters, and in negotiating international forfeiture sharing agreements. Working closely with law enforcement agencies and the United States Attorneys, AFMLS participates and aids in the coordination of domestic and international multi-district investigations and prosecutions. The Section implements DOJ money laundering and asset forfeiture guidelines and provides legal advice and training to the United States Attorney's Offices and investigative agencies.

- The FBI has investigative authority over more than 200 violations of federal law, including money laundering offenses, whether the laundering is related to drug trafficking, terrorism, bank fraud or espionage. The FBI has sole or concurrent jurisdiction in 133 of the 164 "specified unlawful activities" that form predicate crimes for money laundering prosecutions. The FBI gathers and analyzes intelligence data to identify and target the major international and domestic money laundering organizations. In addition, long-term complex undercover money laundering operations are conducted to target the criminal money launderer as well as the underlying criminal activity. The FBI considers money laundering as a principal as well as an ancillary violation that is pursued in all FBI investigations.

- The Justice Department's Special Operations Division is a joint national coordinating and support entity initially comprised of agents and analysts from the DEA, the FBI, the U.S. Customs Service, and prosecutors from the Justice Department's Criminal Division. SOD coordinates and supports regional and national-level criminal investigations and prosecutions against major criminal drug-trafficking organizations. Where appropriate, state and local investigative and prosecutive authorities are fully integrated into SOD-coordinated drug enforcement operations. SOD's financial component, which includes IRS-CI, assembles all available information to identify and target the financial infrastructure of SOD targets, assists in coordinating investigations and prosecutions, and assists in seizing and forfeiting the proceeds, assets, and instrumentalities of these major drug trafficking organizations.

- The DEA is a specialized bureau of the Department of Justice whose sole mission is the enforcement of the U.S. drug trafficking laws. DEA places emphasis on the financial aspects of drug trafficking and works closely with federal, state, local and county law enforcement agencies in money laundering investigations.

Department of State

The Department of State is responsible for the day-to-day liaison with foreign governments on policy matters, including money laundering. Primary responsibility for money laundering matters is vested in the Department's Bureau for International Narcotics and Law Enforcement Affairs (INL), which participates in anti-money laundering initiatives in a variety of ways, including publishing an annual report on international money laundering, helping to coordinate with other agencies intelligence and training and technical assistance on money laundering, and providing considerable funding for international anti-money laundering training. A prime focus of INL's training program is a multi-agency approach to addressing international financial crime, law enforcement development, organized crime fighting, and counternarcotics training. Supported by and in cooperation with INL, the Justice Department, Treasury Department components (i.e., FinCEN and the Office of the Comptroller of the Currency), the Board of Governors of the Federal Reserve, and non-governmental organizations offered law enforcement and criminal justice programs worldwide.

United States Postal Service

The Postal Inspection Service is the investigative arm of the U.S. Postal Service. It has investigative jurisdiction for money laundering in connection with Postal related predicate offences, such as mail fraud. The Postal Inspection Service also investigates money laundering involving the cash purchase of postal money orders, which are often used by money launderers to transport value out of the country.

Office of National Drug Control Policy

The Office of National Drug Control Policy (ONDCP) designates High Intensity Drug Trafficking Areas (HIDTAs) for the purpose of reducing illegal drug trafficking and drug-related crimes and violence in designated high trafficking areas. A significant portion of HIDTA-related efforts is targeted at the laundering of the proceeds of narcotics trafficking. In 1998, Congress reauthorized this ONDCP authority, which is codified at 21 U.S.C. 1706.

Regulatory Compliance

The recordkeeping and reporting requirements of the BSA are a critical component of the counter-money laundering regime. Ensuring that financial institutions and other covered persons and entities comply with these regulatory requirements is the responsibility of a broad range of executive branch and independent agencies including the federal banking regulators, the Securities and Exchange Commission, and the Internal Revenue Service's Examination Division. In addition, other agencies, including the Commodity Futures Trading Commission, assist in this process through the sharing of information and other cooperative efforts.

Federal Banking Regulators

The periodic compliance examinations conducted by the federal banking agencies and regulators -- i.e., the Office of the Comptroller of the Currency; the Office of Thrift Supervision; the Board of Governors of the Federal Reserve System; the Federal Deposit Insurance Corporation; and the National Credit Union Administration -- constitute a very significant deterrent to money laundering. These regulators ensure that institutions that they supervise have in place adequate anti-money laundering internal controls and procedures that include, among other things, procedures to ensure compliance with the reporting and recordkeeping provisions of the BSA and procedures to detect and report suspicious activity. If, in the course of a compliance review, a federal banking regulator detects a suspicious transaction that involves potential money laundering, it ensures that a SAR is filed with FinCEN, either by the bank or by the agency itself. In addition, when a regulator determines that a bank has failed to comply with the reporting requirements of the BSA, it may refer the case to FinCEN for possible civil penalties. The regulators may also pursue administrative enforcement action under the authority provided by 12 U.S.C. 1818.

The Securities and Exchange Commission

The Securities and Exchange Commission (SEC) regulates the U.S. securities markets and market participants, and enforces U.S. securities laws. The SEC also has the statutory responsibility to establish accounting, auditing and independence standards, and to oversee the accounting profession to assure that public company financial statements are prepared and audited utilizing the highest quality accounting, auditing and independence standards. The SEC's chief responsibility with respect to money laundering is to assure compliance with the BSA's reporting, recordkeeping, and record retention obligations by securities brokers and dealers. The SEC investigates and prosecutes securities fraud, which is a predicate offense of money laundering. In monitoring for and taking action against securities fraud, the SEC complements the work of criminal law enforcement authorities in their efforts to combat money laundering.

Internal Revenue Service

The Internal Revenue Service's Examination Division (IRS-Exam) has regulatory authority for civil compliance with the BSA for many non-bank financial institutions (NBFI) such as currency dealers or exchangers, check-cashers, issuers and sellers or redeemers of traveler's checks/money orders or similar monetary instruments, licensed transmitters of funds, telegraph companies, certain casinos and agents/agencies/branches or offices within the United States of banks organized under foreign law. IRS-Exam conducts on-site BSA compliance exams to ensure that NBFIs are in compliance with the reporting, recordkeeping and compliance program requirements of the BSA, and is also responsible for examining and monitoring compliance with the currency reporting requirement on trades and businesses

Commodity Futures Trading Commission

The Commodity Futures Trading Commission (CFTC) is charged with the administration and enforcement of the federal futures and options laws. Although money laundering is not a violation of the laws enforced by the CFTC, it may be accomplished through acts that separately violate these laws – such as wash sales, accommodation trades, fictitious transactions and the filing of false reports – and therefore could result in a CFTC enforcement action.

III.   State and Local Counter-Money Laundering Efforts

The range of activities undertaken at the state and local level to combat money laundering is extensive.

On the enforcement side, 33 states have laws making money laundering a crime. Many of these state laws incorporate, to a varying degree, similar or parallel aspects of federal counter-money laundering laws, including lengthy prison sentences for money laundering (often in the range of 10 to 20 years) and significant criminal fines (e.g., three times the value of the property involved in the transaction). In recent years, there has been an increased focus on investigations involving money laundering and its predicate offenses. Several states have prosecution units that focus on state money laundering prosecutions. These units are composed of a diverse staff including attorneys, investigators, accountants, analysts and computer specialists who have significant expertise in financial investigation techniques and laws relating to money laundering/asset forfeiture. In addition, there are law enforcement task forces in many parts of the country that combine the resources of federal, state and local agencies in combating money laundering and related predicate offences.

States are also actively engaged in the regulation and supervision of financial institutions. Enforcement agencies in all 50 states participate in FinCEN's Project Gateway, which allows authorized users in state law enforcement agencies direct, on-line access to all BSA reports. This program allows states to access individual BSA reports filed anywhere in the country, rather than limiting access to those filed in one particular state. Moreover, several states have enacted currency transaction reporting requirements for bank and non-bank financial institutions that mirror the BSA as a means of collecting data, while several other states receive copies of federal CTRs filed by institutions in their state. And state banking agencies, which share annual BSA compliance audit responsibilities with federal banking regulators for state-chartered banks, review such bank's counter-money laundering efforts.

Appendix 2:
The Forty Recommendations of the
Financial Action Task Force on Money Laundering

Introduction

1.   The Financial Action Task Force on Money Laundering (FATF) is an inter-governmental body whose purpose is the development and promotion of policies to combat money laundering -- the processing of criminal proceeds in order to disguise their illegal origin. These policies aim to prevent such proceeds from being utilised in future criminal activities and from affecting legitimate economic activities.

2.   The FATF currently consists of 26 countries[25] and two international organisations[26]. Its membership includes the major financial centre countries of Europe, North America and Asia. It is a multi-disciplinary body - as is essential in dealing with money laundering - bringing together the policy-making power of legal, financial and law enforcement experts.

3.   This need to cover all relevant aspects of the fight against money laundering is reflected in the scope of the forty FATF Recommendations -- the measures which the Task Force have agreed to implement and which all countries are encouraged to adopt. The Recommendations were originally drawn up in 1990. In 1996 the forty Recommendations were revised to take into account the experience gained over the last six years and to reflect the changes which have occurred in the money laundering problem.[27]

---

[25]   Reference in this document to "countries" should be taken to apply equally to "territories" or "jurisdictions". The twenty six FATF member countries and governments are: Australia, Austria, Belgium, Canada, Denmark, Finland, France, Germany, Greece, Hong Kong, Iceland, Ireland, Italy, Japan, Luxembourg, the Kingdom of the Netherlands, New Zealand, Norway, Portugal, Singapore, Spain, Sweden, Switzerland, Turkey, United Kingdom, and the United States

[26]   The two international organisations are: the European Commission and the Gulf Cooperation Council.

[27]   During the period 1990 to 1995, the FATF also elaborated various Interpretative Notes which are designed to clarify the application of specific Recommendations. Some of these Interpretative Notes have been updated in the Stocktaking Review to reflect changes in the Recommendations.

4.   These forty Recommendations set out the basic framework for anti-money laundering efforts and they are designed to be of universal application. They cover the criminal justice system and law enforcement; the financial system and its regulation, and international cooperation.

5.   It was recognised from the outset of the FATF that countries have diverse legal and financial systems and so all cannot take identical measures. The Recommendations are therefore the principles for action in this field, for countries to implement according to their particular circumstances and constitutional frameworks allowing countries a measure of flexibility rather than prescribing every detail. The measures are not particularly complex or difficult, provided there is the political will to act. Nor do they compromise the freedom to engage in legitimate transactions or threaten economic development.

6.   FATF countries are clearly committed to accept the discipline of being subjected to multilateral surveillance and peer review. All member countries have their implementation of the forty Recommendations monitored through a two-pronged approach: an annual self-assessment exercise and the more detailed mutual evaluation process under which each member country is subject to an on-site examination. In addition, the FATF carries out cross-country reviews of measures taken to implement particular Recommendations.

7.These measures are essential for the creation of an effective anti-money laundering framework.

THE FORTY RECOMMENDATIONS OF THE FINANCIAL ACTION TASK FORCE ON MONEY LAUNDERING

A. GENERAL FRAMEWORK OF THE RECOMMENDATIONS

1. Each country should take immediate steps to ratify and to implement fully, the 1988 United Nations Convention against Illicit Traffic in Narcotic Drugs and Psychotropic Substances (the Vienna Convention).

2. Financial institution secrecy laws should be conceived so as not to inhibit implementation of these recommendations.

3. An effective money laundering enforcement program should include increased multilateral co-operation and mutual legal assistance in money laundering investigations and prosecutions and extradition in money laundering cases, where possible.

B. ROLE OF NATIONAL LEGAL SYSTEMS IN COMBATING MONEY LAUNDERING

Scope of the Criminal Offence of Money Laundering

4. Each country should take such measures as may be necessary, including legislative ones, to enable it to criminalise money laundering as set forth in the Vienna Convention. Each country should extend the offence of drug money laundering to one based on serious offences. Each country would determine which serious crimes would be designated as money laundering predicate offences.

5. As provided in the Vienna Convention, the offence of money laundering should apply at least to knowing money laundering activity, including the concept that knowledge may be inferred from objective factual circumstances.

6. Where possible, corporations themselves - not only their employees - should be subject to criminal liability.

Provisional Measures and Confiscation

7. Countries should adopt measures similar to those set forth in the Vienna Convention, as may be necessary, including legislative ones, to enable their competent authorities to confiscate property laundered, proceeds from, instrumentalities used in or intended for use in the commission of any money laundering offence, or property of corresponding value, without prejudicing the rights of bona fide third parties.

Such measures should include the authority to : 1) identify, trace and evaluate property which is subject to confiscation; 2) carry out provisional measures, such as freezing and seizing, to prevent any dealing, transfer or disposal of such property; and 3) take any appropriate investigative measures.

In addition to confiscation and criminal sanctions, countries also should consider monetary and civil penalties, and/or proceedings including civil proceedings, to void contracts entered into by parties, where parties knew or should have known that as a result of the contract, the State would be prejudiced in its ability to recover financial claims, e.g. through confiscation or collection of fines and penalties.

C. ROLE OF THE FINANCIAL SYSTEM IN COMBATING MONEY LAUNDERING

8. Recommendations 10 to 29 should apply not only to banks, but also to non-bank financial institutions. Even for those non-bank financial institutions which are not subject to a formal prudential supervisory regime in all countries, for example bureaux de change, governments should ensure that these institutions are subject to the same anti-money laundering laws or regulations as all other financial institutions and that these laws or regulations are implemented effectively.

9. The appropriate national authorities should consider applying Recommendations 10 to 21 and 23 to the conduct of financial activities as a commercial undertaking by businesses or professions which are not financial institutions, where such conduct is allowed or not prohibited. Financial activities include, but are not limited to, those listed in the attached annex. It is left to each country to decide whether special situations should be defined where the application of anti-money laundering measures is not necessary, for example, when a financial activity is carried out on an occasional or limited basis.

Customer Identification and Record-keeping Rules

10. Financial institutions should not keep anonymous accounts or accounts in obviously fictitious names: they should be required (by law, by regulations, by agreements between supervisory authorities and financial institutions or by self-regulatory agreements among financial institutions) to identify, on the basis of an official or other reliable identifying document, and record the identity of their clients, either occasional or usual, when establishing business relations or conducting transactions (in particular opening of accounts or passbooks, entering into fiduciary transactions, renting of safe deposit boxes, performing large cash transactions).

In order to fulfill identification requirements concerning legal entities, financial institutions should, when necessary, take measures:

(i) to verify the legal existence and structure of the customer by obtaining either from a public register or from the customer or both, proof of incorporation, including information concerning the customer's name, legal form, address, directors and provisions regulating the power to bind the entity.

(ii) to verify that any person purporting to act on behalf of the customer is so authorised and identify that person.

11. Financial institutions should take reasonable measures to obtain information about the true identity of the persons on whose behalf an account is opened or a transaction conducted if there are any doubts as to whether these clients or customers are acting on their own behalf, for example, in the case of domiciliary companies (i.e. institutions, corporations, foundations, trusts, etc. that do not conduct any commercial or manufacturing business or any other form of commercial operation in the country where their registered office is located).

12. Financial institutions should maintain, for at least five years, all necessary records on transactions, both domestic or international, to enable them to comply swiftly with information requests from the competent authorities. Such records must be sufficient to permit reconstruction of individual transactions (including the amounts and types of currency involved if any) so as to provide, if necessary, evidence for prosecution of criminal behaviour.

Financial institutions should keep records on customer identification (e.g. copies or records of official identification documents like passports, identity cards, driving licenses or similar documents), account files and business correspondence for at least five years after the account is closed.

These documents should be available to domestic competent authorities in the context of relevant criminal prosecutions and investigations.

13. Countries should pay special attention to money laundering threats inherent in new or developing technologies that might favour anonymity, and take measures, if needed, to prevent their use in money laundering schemes.

Increased Diligence of Financial Institutions

14. Financial institutions should pay special attention to all complex, unusual large transactions, and all unusual patterns of transactions, which have no apparent economic or visible lawful purpose. The background and purpose of such transactions should, as far as possible, be examined, the findings established in writing, and be available to help supervisors, auditors and law enforcement agencies.

15. If financial institutions suspect that funds stem from a criminal activity, they should be required to report promptly their suspicions to the competent authorities.

16. Financial institutions, their directors, officers and employees should be protected by legal provisions from criminal or civil liability for breach of any restriction on disclosure of information imposed by contract or by any legislative, regulatory or administrative provision, if they report their suspicions in good faith to the competent authorities, even if they did not know precisely what the underlying criminal activity was, and regardless of whether illegal activity actually occurred.

17. Financial institutions, their directors, officers and employees, should not, or, where appropriate, should not be allowed to, warn their customers when information relating to them is being reported to the competent authorities.

18. Financial institutions reporting their suspicions should comply with instructions from the competent authorities.

19. Financial institutions should develop programs against money laundering. These programs should include, as a minimum :

    (lxx)   the development of internal policies, procedures and controls, including the designation of compliance officers at management level, and adequate screening procedures to ensure high standards when hiring employees;

    (lxxi)   an ongoing employee training programme;

    (lxxii)   an audit function to test the system.

Measures to Cope with the Problem of Countries with No or Insufficient Anti-Money Laundering Measures

20. Financial institutions should ensure that the principles mentioned above are also applied to branches and majority owned subsidiaries located abroad, especially in countries which do not or insufficiently apply these Recommendations, to the extent that local applicable laws and regulations permit. When local applicable laws and regulations prohibit this implementation, competent authorities in the country of the mother institution should be informed by the financial institutions that they cannot apply these Recommendations.

21. Financial institutions should give special attention to business relations and transactions with persons, including companies and financial institutions, from countries which do not or insufficiently apply these Recommendations. Whenever these transactions have no apparent economic or visible lawful purpose, their background and purpose should, as far as possible, be examined, the findings established in writing, and be available to help supervisors, auditors and law enforcement agencies.

Other Measures to Avoid Money Laundering

22. Countries should consider implementing feasible measures to detect or monitor the physical cross-border transportation of cash and bearer negotiable instruments, subject to strict safeguards to ensure proper use of information and without impeding in any way the freedom of capital movements.

23. Countries should consider the feasibility and utility of a system where banks and other financial institutions and intermediaries would report all domestic and international currency transactions above a fixed amount, to a national central agency with a computerised data base, available to competent authorities for use in money laundering cases, subject to strict safeguards to ensure proper use of the information.

24. Countries should further encourage in general the development of modern and secure techniques of money management, including increased use of checks, payment cards, direct deposit of salary checks, and book entry recording of securities, as a means to encourage the replacement of cash transfers.

25. Countries should take notice of the potential for abuse of shell corporations by money launderers and should consider whether additional measures are required to prevent unlawful use of such entities.

Implementation, and Role of Regulatory and other Administrative Authorities

26. The competent authorities supervising banks or other financial institutions or intermediaries, or other competent authorities, should ensure that the supervised institutions have adequate programs to guard against money laundering. These authorities should co-operate and lend expertise spontaneously or on request with other domestic judicial or law enforcement authorities in money laundering investigations and prosecutions.

27. Competent authorities should be designated to ensure an effective implementation of all these Recommendations, through administrative supervision and regulation, in other professions dealing with cash as defined by each country.

28. The competent authorities should establish guidelines which will assist financial institutions in detecting suspicious patterns of behaviour by their customers. It is understood that such guidelines must develop over time, and will never be exhaustive. It is further understood that such guidelines will primarily serve as an educational tool for financial institutions' personnel.

29. The competent authorities regulating or supervising financial institutions should take the necessary legal or regulatory measures to guard against control or acquisition of a significant participation in

financial institutions by criminals or their confederates.

D. STRENGTHENING OF INTERNATIONAL CO-OPERATION

Administrative Co-operation

Exchange of general information

30. National administrations should consider recording, at least in the aggregate, international flows of cash in whatever currency, so that estimates can be made of cash flows and reflows from various sources abroad, when this is combined with central bank information. Such information should be made available to the International Monetary Fund and the Bank for International Settlements to facilitate international studies.

31. International competent authorities, perhaps Interpol and the World Customs Organisation, should be given responsibility for gathering and disseminating information to competent authorities about the latest developments in money laundering and money laundering techniques. Central banks and bank regulators could do the same on their network. National authorities in various spheres, in consultation with trade associations, could then disseminate this to financial institutions in individual countries.

Exchange of information relating to suspicious transactions

32. Each country should make efforts to improve a spontaneous or "upon request" international information exchange relating to suspicious transactions, persons and corporations involved in those transactions between competent authorities. Strict safeguards should be established to ensure that this exchange of information is consistent with national and international provisions on privacy and data protection.

Other forms of Co-operation

Basis and means for co-operation in confiscation, mutual assistance and extradition

33. Countries should try to ensure, on a bilateral or multilateral basis, that different knowledge standards in national definitions - i.e. different standards concerning the intentional element of the infraction - do not affect the ability or willingness of countries to provide each other with mutual legal assistance.

34. International co-operation should be supported by a network of bilateral and multilateral agreements and arrangements based on generally shared legal concepts with the aim of providing practical measures to affect the widest possible range of mutual assistance.

35. Countries should be encouraged to ratify and implement relevant international conventions on money laundering such as the 1990 Council of Europe Convention on Laundering, Search, Seizure and Confiscation of the Proceeds from Crime.

Focus of improved mutual assistance on money laundering issues

36. Co-operative investigations among countries' appropriate competent authorities should be encouraged. One valid and effective investigative technique in this respect is controlled delivery related to assets known or suspected to be the proceeds of crime. Countries are encouraged to support this technique, where possible.

37. There should be procedures for mutual assistance in criminal matters regarding the use of compulsory measures including the production of records by financial institutions and other persons, the search of persons and premises, seizure and obtaining of evidence for use in money laundering investigations and prosecutions and in related actions in foreign jurisdictions.

38. There should be authority to take expeditious action in response to requests by foreign countries to identify, freeze, seize and confiscate proceeds or other property of corresponding value to such proceeds, based on money laundering or the crimes underlying the laundering activity. There should also be arrangements for coordinating seizure and confiscation proceedings which may include the sharing of confiscated assets.

39. To avoid conflicts of jurisdiction, consideration should be given to devising and applying mechanisms for determining the best venue for prosecution of defendants in the interests of justice in cases that are subject to prosecution in more than one country. Similarly, there should be arrangements for coordinating seizure and confiscation proceedings which may include the sharing of confiscated assets.

40. Countries should have procedures in place to extradite, where possible, individuals charged with a money laundering offence or related offences. With respect to its national legal system, each country should recognise money laundering as an extraditable offence. Subject to their legal frameworks, countries may consider simplifying extradition by allowing direct transmission of extradition requests between appropriate ministries, extraditing persons based only on warrants of arrests or judgements, extraditing their nationals, and/or introducing a simplified extradition of consenting persons who waive formal extradition proceedings.

Annex to Recommendation 9: List of Financial Activities undertaken by business or professions which are not financial institutions

1.   Acceptance of deposits and other repayable funds from the public.
2.   Lending.[1]
3.   Financial leasing.
4.   Money transmission services.
5.   Issuing and managing means of payment (e.g. credit and debit cards, cheques, traveller's cheques and bankers' drafts...).
6.   Financial guarantees and commitments.
7.   Trading for account of customers (spot, forward, swaps, futures, options...) in:
>   (a) money market instruments (cheques, bills, CDs, etc.) ;
>   (b) foreign exchange;
>   (c) exchange, interest rate and index instruments;
>   (d) transferable securities;
>   (e) commodity futures trading.
8.   Participation in securities issues and the provision of financial services related to such   issues.
9.   Individual and collective portfolio management.
10.   Safekeeping and administration of cash or liquid securities on behalf of clients.
11.   Life insurance and other investment related insurance.
12.   Money changing.

---

[1]   Including inter alia

- consumer credit
- mortgage credit
- factoring, with or without recourse
- finance of commercial transactions (including forfaiting)

Appendix 3:
The Twenty-Five FATF Criteria For Determining Non-Cooperative Countries and Territories

A. Loopholes in financial regulations

(i) No or inadequate regulations and supervision of financial institutions

1. Absence or ineffective regulations and supervision for all financial institutions in a given country or territory, onshore or offshore, on an equivalent basis with respect to international standards applicable to money laundering.

(ii) Inadequate licensing and creation rules for financial institutions, including assessing the backgrounds of their managers and beneficial owners

2. Possibility for individuals or legal entities to operate a financial institution without authorisation or registration or with very rudimentary requirements for authorisation or registration.

3. Absence of measures to guard against holding of management functions and control or acquisition of a significant investment in financial institutions by criminals or their confederates.

(iii) Inadequate customer identification requirements for financial institutions

4. Existence of anonymous accounts or accounts in obviously fictitious names.

5. Lack of effective laws, regulations, agreements between supervisory authorities and financial institutions or self-regulatory agreements among financial institutions on identification by the financial institution of the client and beneficial owner of an account:

– no obligation to verify the identity of the client;
– no requirement to identify the beneficial owners where there are doubts as to whether the client is acting on his own behalf;
– no obligation to renew identification of the client or the beneficial owner when doubts appear as to their identity in the course of business relationships;
- no requirement for financial institutions to develop ongoing anti-money laundering training programmes.

6. Lack of a legal or regulatory obligation for financial institutions or agreements between supervisory authorities and financial institutions or self-agreements among financial institutions to record

and keep, for a reasonable and sufficient time (five years), documents connected with the identity of their clients, as well as records on national and international transactions.

7.   Legal or practical obstacles to access by administrative and judicial authorities to information with respect to the identity of the holders or beneficial owners and information connected with the transactions recorded.

(iv) Excessive secrecy provisions regarding financial institutions

8.   Secrecy provisions which can be invoked against, but not lifted by competent administrative authorities in the context of enquiries concerning money laundering.

9.   Secrecy provisions which can be invoked against, but not lifted by judicial authorities in criminal investigations related to money laundering.

(v) Lack of efficient suspicious transactions reporting system

10.   Absence of an efficient mandatory system for reporting suspicious or unusual transactions to a competent authority, provided that such a system aims to detect and prosecute money laundering.

11.   Lack of monitoring and criminal or administrative sanctions in respect to the obligation to report suspicious or unusual transactions.

B.   **Obstacles raised by other regulatory requirements**

(i) Inadequate commercial law requirements for registration of business and legal entities

12.   Inadequate means for identifying, recording and making available relevant information related to legal and business entities (name, legal form, address, identity of directors, provisions regulating the power to bind the entity).

(ii) Lack of identification of the beneficial owner(s) of legal and business entities

13.   Obstacles to identification by financial institutions of the beneficial owner(s) and directors/officers of a company or beneficiaries of legal or business entities.

14.   Regulatory or other systems which allow financial institutions to carry out financial business where the beneficial owners of transactions is unknown, or is represented by an intermediary who refuses to divulge that information, without informing the competent authorities.

C.   Obstacles to international co-operation

(i) Obstacles to international co-operation by administrative authorities

15.   Laws or regulations prohibiting international exchange of information between administrative anti-money laundering authorities or not granting clear gateways or subjecting exchange of information to unduly restrictive conditions.

16.   Prohibiting relevant administrative authorities to conduct investigations or enquiries on behalf or for account of their foreign counterparts.

17.   Obvious unwillingness to respond constructively to requests (e.g. failure to take the appropriate measures in due course, long delays in responding).

18.   Restrictive practices in international co-operation against money laundering between supervisory authorities or between FIUs for the analysis and investigation of suspicious transactions, especially on the grounds that such transactions may relate to tax matters.

(ii) Obstacles to international co-operation by judicial authorities

19.   Failure to criminalise laundering of the proceeds from serious crimes.

20.   Laws or regulations prohibiting international exchange of information between judicial authorities (notably specific reservations to the anti-money laundering provisions of international agreements) or placing highly restrictive conditions on the exchange of information.

21.   Obvious unwillingness to respond constructively to mutual legal assistance requests (e.g. failure to take the appropriate measures in due course, long delays in responding).

22.   Refusal to provide judicial co-operation in cases involving offences recognised as such by the requested jurisdiction especially on the grounds that tax matters are involved.

D.   Inadequate resources for preventing and detecting money laundering activities

(i) Lack of resources in public and private sectors

23.   Failure to provide the administrative and judicial authorities with the necessary financial, human or technical resources to exercise their functions or to conduct their investigations.

24.   Inadequate or corrupt professional staff in either governmental, judicial or supervisory authorities or among those responsible for anti-money laundering compliance in the financial services industry.

(ii) Absence of a financial intelligence unit or of an equivalent mechanism

25.   Lack of a centralised unit (i.e., a financial intelligence unit) or of an equivalent mechanism for the collection, analysis and dissemination of suspicious transactions information to competent authorities.

Appendix 4:

The G-7's Ten Key Principles for the Improvement of International Cooperation Regarding Financial Crime and Regulatory Abuse

The Denver Summit remitted countries to take steps to improve international co-operation between law enforcement authorities and financial regulators on cases involving serious financial crime and regulatory abuse. In making these improvements, and seeking to improve spontaneous and "upon request" international information exchange in this field, countries should adhere to the key principles set out below.

While remaining consistent with fundamental national and international legal principles and essential national interests, countries should:

(1)   ensure that their laws and systems provide for the maximum cooperation <u>domestically</u> between financial regulators and law enforcement authorities in both directions. In particular, when financial regulators identify suspected financial crime activity in supervised institutions or financial markets, they should share this information with law enforcement authorities or, if applicable, the national Financial Intelligence Unit;

(2)   ensure that there are clear definitions of the role, duty, and obligations of all the national authorities involved in tackling illicit financial activity;

(3)   provide accessible and transparent channels for cooperation and exchange of information on financial crime and regulatory abuse at the <u>international level,</u> including effective and efficient gateways for the provision of information. Instruments such as Memoranda of Understanding and Mutual Legal Assistance Treaties can be very valuable in setting out the framework for co-operation but their absence should not preclude the exchange of information;

(4)   at the international level, either introduce or expand <u>direct</u> exchange of information between law enforcement authorities and financial regulators or ensure that the quality of national cooperation between law enforcement authorities and financial regulators permits a fast and efficient <u>indirect</u> exchange of information;

(5)   ensure that law enforcement authorities and financial regulators are able to supply information at the international level spontaneously as well as in response to requests and actively encourage this where it would support further action against financial crime and regulatory abuse;

(6)   provide that their laws and systems enable foreign financial regulators and law enforcement authorities with whom information on financial crimes or regulatory abuse is shared

to use the information for the full range of their responsibilities subject to any necessary limitations established at the outset;

(7)   provide that foreign financial regulators and law enforcement authorities with whom information on financial crimes or regulatory abuse is shared are permitted, with prior consent, to pass the information on for regulatory or law enforcement purposes to other such authorities in that jurisdiction. Proper account should be taken of established channels of co-operation, such as mutual legal assistance statutes and treaties, judicial co-operation, Memoranda of Understanding, or informal arrangements;

(8)   provide that their law enforcement authorities and financial regulators maintain the confidentiality of information received from a foreign authority within the framework of key principles 6 and 7, using the information only for the purposes stated in the original request, or as otherwise agreed, and observing any limitations imposed on its supply. Where an authority wishes to use the information for purposes other than those originally stated or as otherwise previously agreed, it will seek the prior consent of the foreign authority;

(9)   ensure that the arrangements for supplying information within regulatory and law enforcement cooperation framework are as fast , effective and transparent as possible. Where information cannot be shared, parties should as appropriate discuss the reasons with one another;

(10)   keep their laws and procedures relating to international cooperation on financial crimes and regulatory abuse under review to ensure that, where circumstances change and improvements can be made, an appropriate response can be implemented as quickly as possible.

Appendix 5:
Goals, Objectives and Action Items of the
2000 National Money Laundering Strategy

Goal 1:   Strengthening Domestic Enforcement To Disrupt the Flow of Illicit Money

Objective 1:   Concentrate Resources in High-Risk Areas

Action Item 1.1.1: The Departments of the Treasury and Justice will oversee specially-designed counter-money laundering efforts in each newly designated HIFCA.

Action Item 1.1.2: The Treasury Department in consultation with the Department of Justice will continue the process of evaluating and designating HIFCAs.

Objective 2:   Communicate Money Laundering Priorities to Federal Law Enforcement in the Field

Action Item 1.2.1: The Departments of the Treasury and Justice will track implementation by investigators and prosecutors of the joint memorandum.

Objective 3:   Seek Legislation Enhancing Money Laundering Enforcement

Action Item 1.3.1: The Administration will seek enactment of the Money Laundering Act of 2000 (formerly the Money Laundering Act of 1999), legislation with powerful provisions addressing domestic money laundering enforcement.

Action Item 1.3.2: The Administration will seek legislative authority for the Customs Service to search outbound mail.

Objective 4:   Examine the Relationship between Money Laundering and Tax Evasion.

Action Item 1.4.1: The Departments of the Treasury and Justice will study whether it would be advisable to expand the list of money laundering predicates to include tax offenses.

Objective 5:   Enhance Inter-agency Coordination of Money Laundering Investigations

Action Item 1.5.1: The Justice Department will continue to enhance the capacity of the Special Operations Division (SOD) to contribute to financial investigations in narcotics cases.

Action Item 1.5.2: The Customs Service will make the Money Laundering Coordination Center (MLCC) fully operational with the participation of all relevant law enforcement agencies.

Action Item 1.5.3: The Department of Justice will enhance the money laundering focus of counter-drug task forces.

Action Item 1.5.4: The Treasury Department will evaluate areas or financial sectors where use of Geographic Targeting Orders (GTOs) may be appropriate.

Objective 6:   Identify and Target Major Money Laundering Systems

Action Item 1.6.1: The Department of Treasury will intensify and expand efforts to increase the business community's education and awareness of the Black Market Peso Exchange System.

Action Item 1.6.2: Law Enforcement Agencies, working in conjunction with the Money Laundering Coordination Center, will continue to identify the methods used for placement of peso exchange funds into the financial system.

Action Item 1.6.3: The Money Laundering Coordination Center will enhance coordination of investigative efforts against the peso exchange system.

Action Item 1.6.4: The Administration will promote continued cooperation with the Governments of Colombia, Aruba, Panama, and Venezuela.

Objective 7:   Enhance the Collection, Analysis, and Sharing of Information to Target Money Launderers

Action Item 1.7.1: The Departments of the Treasury and Justice will ensure that their bureaus provide feedback to FinCEN on the use of SARs and other BSA information.

Action Item 1.7.2: The Departments of the Treasury and Justice will review available technologies to determine the utility of developing a uniform procedure for conducting document exploitation.

Objective 8:   Intensify Training

Action Item 1.8.1: The Departments of the Treasury and Justice will continue to sponsor national and regional money laundering conferences.

Objective 9:   *Continue to Improve the Efficiency and Effectiveness of Resource Management Related to Anti-Money Laundering Efforts.*

Action Item 1.9.1: Under the guidance of OMB, the interagency community will undertake a thorough review of resources devoted to anti-money laundering efforts.

Goal 2:   **Enhancing Regulatory and Cooperative Public-Private Efforts to Prevent Money Laundering**

Objective 1:   *Enhance the Defenses of U.S. Financial Institutions Against Abuse by Criminal Organizations*

Action Item 2.1.1: The Departments of the Treasury and Justice, and the federal bank regulators, will work closely with the financial services industry to develop guidance for financial institutions to conduct enhanced scrutiny of those customers and their transactions that pose a heightened risk of money laundering and other financial crimes.

Action Item 2.1.2: The federal bank supervisory agencies will implement the results of their 180-day review of existing bank examination procedures relating to the prevention and detection of money laundering at financial organizations.

Objective 2:   *Assure that All Types of Financial Institutions Are Subject to Effective Bank Secrecy Act Requirements*

Action Item 2.2.1: The Treasury Department will begin the process to ensure that money services businesses (MSBs) are educated about their obligations under the new rule requiring their registration and the reporting of suspicious activity.

Action Item 2.2.2: The Treasury Department will issue a final rule for the reporting of suspicious activity by casinos and card clubs.

Action Item 2.2.3: The Treasury Department will work with the SEC to propose rules for the reporting of suspicious activity by brokers and dealers in securities.

Action Item 2.2.4: The IRS will enhance the resources devoted to conducting BSA examinations of MSBs and casinos.

Action Item 2.2.5: The Treasury Department will examine the money laundering vulnerabilities of the financial services provider industries not addressed in the *Strategy* -- such as the insurance industry, travel agencies, and pawn brokers -- and recommend, as appropriate, application of BSA requirements.

Objective 3:   *Continue to Strengthen Counter-Money Laundering Efforts of Federal and State Financial Regulators*

Action Item 2.3.1: The Departments of the Treasury and Justice and the federal financial regulators will issue a joint memorandum identifying measures for the enhanced sharing of information between law enforcement and regulatory authorities.

Action Item 2.3.2: The Departments of the Treasury and Justice and the federal financial regulators will begin regular meetings of senior law enforcement and regulatory officials to discuss counter-money laundering efforts in each regulatory district throughout the nation.

Action Item 2.3.3: The Departments of the Treasury and Justice and the federal financial regulators will expand training opportunities for federal financial investigators and bank examiners.

Objective 4:   *Increase Usefulness of Reported Information to Reporting Institutions*

Action Item 2.4.1: FinCEN will continue to expand the flow to banks of information based on SARs and other BSA reports, and on the utility of these reports to law enforcement.

Objective 5:   *Work in Partnership with Associations of Legal and Financial Professionals to Ensure that Money Launderers are Denied Access to the Financial System.*

Action Item 2.5.1: A study group consisting of the Departments of the Treasury and Justice, FinCEN, the SEC, the federal bank regulators will examine how best to utilize accountants and auditors in the detection and deterrence of money laundering.

Action Item 2.5.2: Review the professional responsibilities of lawyers and accountants with regard to money laundering and make recommendations -- ranging from enhanced professional education, standards or rules, to legislation -- as might be needed.

Objective 6:   *Ensure that Regulatory Efforts to Prevent Money Laundering Are Responsive to the Continuing Development of New Technologies*

Action Item 2.6.1: The Departments of the Treasury and Justice and the federal financial regulators will continue outreach to the private sector to ensure that anti-money laundering safeguards respond to new technologies.

Action Item 2.6.2: The Departments of the Treasury and Justice, and the federal financial regulators, will examine existing legal authorities with respect to stored value cards to determine whether current law is adequate in addressing their potential use in money laundering.

Objective 7:   *Understand Implications of Counter-Money Laundering Programs for Personal Privacy*

> Action Item 2.7.1: The Treasury Department's working group on personal privacy and money laundering will continue its review of counter-money laundering and privacy policies, and will recommend modifications to existing counter-money laundering laws and regulations, as necessary, to enhance the protection of personal information obtained to carry out these counter-money laundering programs.

Goal 3:   **Strengthening Partnerships With State and Local Governments to Fight Money Laundering Throughout the United States**

Objective 1:   *Provide Seed Capital for State and Local Counter-Money Laundering Enforcement Efforts*

> Action Item 3.1.1: The Departments of the Treasury and Justice will accept applications and award grants under the C-FIC program.

Objective 2:   *Promote the Free Flow of Relevant Information Between State and Federal Enforcement Efforts*

> Action Item 3.2.1: The Departments of the Treasury and Justice will reach out to state and local authorities broadly for contributions to the *National Money Laundering Strategy*, to ensure that federal priorities are consistent with and complementary to state and local strategies.

> Action Item 3.2.2: The Department of the Treasury will promote the use of FinCEN's Gateway Program as a vehicle for two-way information exchange and joint state-federal financial analysis projects.

Objective 3:   *Encourage Comprehensive State Counter-Money Laundering and Related Legislation*

> Action Item 3.3.1: The Departments of the Treasury and Justice will provide technical assistance for enhanced state laws against money laundering.

Objective 4:   *Support Enhanced Training for State and Local Investigators and Prosecutors*

> Action Item 3.4.1: The Departments of the Treasury and Justice will complete revision of a model curriculum for a financial investigations course for state and local law enforcement agencies, hold "Train the Trainer" national conferences, and distribute the curriculum.

Goal 4:   Strengthening International Cooperation to Disrupt the Global Flow of Illicit Money

Objective 1:   Seek Legislation Enhancing the Government's Ability to Protect U.S. Institutions and the U.S. Financial System from International Money Laundering.

Action Item 4.1.1: The Administration will seek enactment of the International Counter-Money Laundering Act of 2000.

Objective 2:   Apply increasing pressure on jurisdictions where lax controls invite money laundering.

Action Item 4.2.1: Identify jurisdictions that pose a money laundering threat to the United States.

Sub-Action Item 4.2.1.a: The United States will complete an internal evaluation of financial crime havens.

Sub-Action Item 4.2.1.b: Support the on-going efforts of FATF to identify non-cooperative jurisdictions based upon its twenty-five criteria.

Sub-Action Item 4.2.1.c: Support efforts of the Financial Stability Forum (FSF) and regional fora in urging countries and jurisdictions to adopt and adhere to international anti-money laundering standards.

Sub-Action Item 4.2.1.d: Support multilateral efforts to identify tax havens.

Action Item 4.2.2: Take appropriate action with respect to identified financial crime havens.

Sub-Action Item 4.2.2.a: The U.S. will take appropriate action in support of multilateral efforts.

Sub-Action Item 4.2.2.b: Promote adoption of supervisory and regulatory actions -- such as increased regulatory reporting, increased external and internal audits, differentiated risk treatment -- in response to specified jurisdictions that fail to make progress in implementing effective international standards relating to money laundering.

Sub-Action Item 4.2.2.c: Issue bank advisories when appropriate.

Sub-Action Item 4.2.2.d: Implement the Foreign Narcotics Kingpin Designation Act and consider using IEEPA powers to target narcotics-related money launderers in other appropriate circumstances.

Objective 3:   Continue to Work with Countries to Adopt and Adhere to International Money Laundering Standards

Action Item 4.3.1: Work toward universal implementation of the FATF 40 Recommendations.

Action Item 4.3.2: Promote the development of FATF-style regional bodies.

Action Item 4.3.3: Negotiate strong anti-money laundering provisions in the pending United Nations Convention against Transnational Organized Crime.

Action Item 4.3.4: The United States will continue to urge the international financial institutions (IFIs) to explore mechanisms to encourage and support countries, in the context of financial sector reform programs, to adopt anti-money laundering policies and measures.

Action Item 4.3.5: Enhance the provision of training and assistance to nations making efforts to implement counter-money laundering measures.

Action Item 4.3.6: Support and expand membership of the Egmont Group of financial intelligence units.

Objective 4:   Advance the International Fight Against Corruption.

Action Item 4.4.1: Expand the list of money laundering predicates under U.S. law to include numerous foreign crimes, including public corruption, not currently covered by the money laundering statute.

Action Item 4.4.2: Urge other nations to make public corruption a predicate offense under their own anti-money laundering statutes.

Action Item 4.4.3: The Treasury Department, working in cooperation with the Departments of State and Justice, will coordinate an interagency effort to examine the problem of foreign government officials who make use of the international financial system to convert public assets to their personal use.

Sub-Action Item 4.4.3.a: The Departments of the Treasury, State, and Justice will review the tools and methodologies available to identify, trace and seize stolen assets of other countries (in particular how the international financial system is used to launder these assets) and make recommendations, as necessary, for enhancements or additional authorities.

Objective 5:   Develop and Support Additional Multilateral Efforts to Facilitate Information Sharing.

Action Item 4.5.1: Urge the G-7 nations to consider an initiative to harmonize rules relating to international funds transfers so that the originators of the transfers will be identified.

Action Item 4.5.2: Expand law enforcement information exchange and judicial cooperation channels.

Action Item 4.5.3: Create an interagency team from FinCEN, the Federal Reserve Board, Treasury, Justice and other appropriate agencies, to promote understanding of mechanisms and processes associated with the movement of criminal proceeds into, through and out of the United States and among other at-risk nations.

Objective 6:   Improve Coordination and Effectiveness of International Enforcement Efforts.

Action Item 4.6.1: The Departments of the Treasury, State, and Justice will work together to enhance information sharing on known or suspected alien money launderers to facilitate the denial or revocation of visas held by such persons.

Objective 7:   Build Knowledge and Understanding

Action Item 4.7.1: Continue to advance the work on estimating the magnitude of money laundering.

Action Item 4.7.2: The Departments of the Treasury and Justice, and the federal financial regulators, will assess the implications for money laundering of the increasing availability through the Internet of financial services offered to U.S. persons by foreign financial service providers.

Action Item 4.7.3: Continue to examine the nature of correspondent banking accounts and other international financial mechanisms, such as payable through accounts, private banking, and wire transfers, and determine the nature and extent of their susceptibility to abuse by money launderers.

INSERT APPENDIX 6

Consultations

Officials of the following agencies were consulted in the drafting of the National Money Laundering Strategy:

Commodity Futures Trading Commission
Department of Justice
    -- Asset Forfeiture and Money Laundering Section
    -- Criminal Division
    -- Tax Division
Department of State
Drug Enforcement Administration
Federal Bureau of Investigation
Federal Deposit Insurance Corporation
Federal Reserve Board
Financial Crimes Enforcement Network
Internal Revenue Service
National Security Council
National Credit Union Administration
Office of the Comptroller of the Currency
Office of National Drug Control Policy
Office of Thrift Supervision
United States Customs Service
United States Postal Inspection Service
United States Secret Service
United States Securities and Exchange Commission

www.ingramcontent.com/pod-product-compliance
Lightning Source LLC
Chambersburg PA
CBHW080259180526
45167CB00006B/2595